DID I JUST SAY THAT?

The Powerful Influence of Words

JEFF BELL

WESTBOW°
PRESS
A DIVISION OF THOMAS NELSON
& ZONDERVAN

WestBow Press books may be ordered through booksellers or by contacting:

WestBow Press
A Division of Thomas Nelson & Zondervan
1663 Liberty Drive
Bloomington, IN 47403
www.westbowpress.com
1 (866) 928-1240

ISBN: 978-1-4908-8795-1 (sc)
ISBN: 978-1-4908-8796-8 (hc)
ISBN: 978-1-4908-8797-5 (e)

Library of Congress Control Number: 2015913371

Print information available on the last page.

WestBow Press rev. date: 07/27/2015

ACKNOWLEDGEMENTS

A SPECIAL THANKS TO MY WONDERFUL wife, Tammy, and my daughter, Brianna, who were very patient and supportive of me in the process of writing this book, and who were willing to sacrifice their time with me so I could finish it.

A special thanks to Steve Barnes, my spiritual advisor, who assisted me with ideas for the book and was my prayer partner as I sought God for wisdom throughout this project.

And finally I want to thank my church family for their constant words of encouragement that inspired me to complete the book and to all those who made special donations for the publishing of the book.

TABLE OF CONTENTS

FOREWORD

ODAY'S HIGHLY DIGITAL AND FAST paced society enables a person's thoughts to make its way to the entire world within seconds. Just ask Rebecca Marino, who is in her early twenties, announced her retirement from the professional sport because she has been lambasted by negative comments from people via social media. After six years of struggling with depression, the result of hundreds of careless comments was Marino calling it quits to a life-long dream.

We live in a culture that knows no boundaries, no thought of consequence when it comes to voicing personal opinion. Political lobbyists battle daily for the rights of freedom of speech and opinions are like noses, everybody has one. Teen suicides related to cyber bullying are at an all time high and continue to climb. Television has turned from good family entertainment to who can one-up the other person with the better putdown line, an attempt to elevate one person by demeaning another. When should the right to freedom of speech be balanced with the responsibility of the communicator to use wisdom and good judgment with a keen understanding for what is best for all who are engaged in communication?

If the hope of our nation's future is going to be bright and promising for generations to come, we must place a high value on others and follow that old Golden Rule by treating others as we would treat ourselves. In *Did I Just Say That*, author Jeff Bell takes us back to the root of it all, the use of our words. Jeff teaches the importance of thinking before we communicate whether verbally or in written form and just as important, how we speak to our self. Like a trained and experienced rider on a horse, Jeff Bell will teach you practical steps to bridling the strongest muscle in your body, the tongue. Learning to do this will change the outlook of your future and those around you by speaking life into what could otherwise be left as a very dark place.

In Proverbs chapter eighteen verse twenty one, the Bible says, *"Death and life are in the power of the tongue,"* nothing could be truer. By applying the nuggets of truth found in the pages of this helpful resource Jeff Bell will positively transform your life and the lives of those around you by coaching you to communicate effectively and minimize the number of times you find yourself asking *"did I just that?"*

Rev. Steve Barnes
President and Founder, Church X2.org

INTRODUCTION

THERE ARE MANY THINGS THAT can influence us; some have a good influence on us while others a bad influence. It is how we utilize what is at our disposal that will determine its influence. Not utilizing things wisely will have a bad influence on our life and hinder us more than help us. It's rightly applying what is at our disposal that will lead to a positive influence.

Such is the case with the words we speak. We all have words at our disposal each day to speak, but what determines whether those words have a positive influence is how we use them.

Proverbs 18:21 tells us that death and life are in the power of the tongue. Our words have the power to build people up or to tear them down, to bring death to a vision or life to a vision, to promote unity or disunity, to communicate happiness or create sorrow. A familiar idiom says, "Sticks and stones may break my bones, but words will never hurt me." It is true that sticks and stones can break bones, but words can kill. Truly there is influence in our words—either for good or for bad.

The fact is there are so many words that we speak during the day that we may not always be aware of the influence those words have. We speak to our wife and children before we leave the house for work, we speak to our coworkers at work, we speak to the waitress at lunch time, we speak to people at church, we speak to our pets, and some of us may even talk to ourselves. All the while we are speaking forth those words; they become more than just words to those who hear them. Many times we can see the influence our words have by looking at the reactions people give us such as their facial expressions and gestures.

But most people probably do not notice the influence their words have, whether for good or for bad, nor do they realize the importance of the words they speak. It's because of this powerful influence of words on ourselves and others that I was compelled to write this book.

In the process of writing this book, I examined the use of my own words and the influence of those words on myself and others. As a result, I have been more careful in how I state things and have seen in my own life the powerful influence that words can have when stated appropriately.

Many of the chapters in this book are taken from stories in the Bible, which make them more relatable. It's always been amazing to me how one can read a story from the Old Testament and the principles in that story are still relevant for today. I have also added many of my own life experiences to make it more personable.

To reinforce what you have learned, there are Challenge Questions at the end of each chapter that can be used also for Bible studies.

It's my hope that your reading of this book will have the same impact on your life that it has had on mine as I wrote it. If you read this book with an open heart, I believe that you will come away with nuggets of wisdom that will enable you to be more effective with the words that you speak. You will discover how important your words are and the appropriate ways to speak those words so that they have a positive influence on yourself and others.

Chapter 1

YOUR STRONGEST MUSCLE
James 3:1-12

T HE THIRD CHAPTER OF JAMES expounds on the influence of our words. In these verses, the writer details the importance of the tongue, a small yet powerful member of the human body.

It's not always the case that the biggest things are always the most powerful; there are many small things that can also pack a lot of power. It's amazing in the technology available how much smaller things have gotten such as computers but yet how much more powerful they are in their ability to process information and store data. Race cars are not big vehicles when compared with vans or trucks, but they are much more powerful in the speed and force that they can generate. There is a saying that it is not the size of the dog in the fight, but rather the size of the fight in the dog that determines which dog wins the fight.

The tongue is one of the smallest members of the human body yet it is considered by many to be the most powerful. Relative to its size, the tongue is the strongest muscle in the body. It is made up of groups of muscles and is always continually working, just like the heart. It binds and contorts to help us speak. Even when one is sleeping, it is pushing saliva down the throat. It is said that the tongue can lift up to eighty times its own weight.

To the physician, the tongue is merely a two ounce slab of mucous membrane enclosing a complex array of muscles and nerves that enable us to chew, taste, and swallow. Equally significant, it is the major organ of communication that enables us to articulate distinct sounds so we can understand one another.

The physician usually begins a physical examination by telling his patient, "Stick out your tongue." Medical science has learned that the tongue serves as an index of the body. An unhealthy tongue means an unhealthy body. A healthy tongue, a healthy body. What is true of the body is true of the soul. A tongue of scorn is a sick soul. A tongue of praise is a healthy soul. Death and life are in the power of the tongue.

In this chapter, we will learn of the power of this small member to influence the course of one's life.

Directs the Course of One's Life

James 3:1-5a says, "Not many of you should become teachers, my fellow believers, because you know that we who teach will be judged more strictly. We all stumble in many ways. Anyone who is never at fault in what they say is perfect, able to keep their whole body in check. When we put bits into the mouths of horses to make them obey us, we can turn the whole animal. Or take ships as an example. Although they are so large and are driven by strong winds, they are steered by a very small rudder wherever the pilot wants to go. Likewise, the tongue is a small part of the body, but it makes great boasts . . ."

It is vital how we use this little member, the tongue, because of its ability to offend. This is why the writer admonished his readers to not seek to be teachers if they were not qualified to do so since public speaking would be involved and there would be more possibility of offending people with their words. They were caught up in the prestige of being a teacher but had forgotten about the tremendous responsibility and accountability.

Such is the challenge to not err with our words that the writer says the man who is never at fault with his words is a perfect man. He is perfect in the sense that he is able to keep every other member of his body in subjection and not prone to err in other things. This is true because it is the tongue that leads to deeds. Since the tongue is the vehicle by which man expresses his thoughts and emotions, when this little member is kept under proper restraint, then all the other members of the body are as easily controlled. Thus, the man who can discipline his tongue gives evidence that he can control his whole body. He proves that he is a mature (perfect) man.

In verses 3–5a, James presents two items that are small of themselves, yet exercise great power, just like the tongue.

First, he makes mention of a small bit that is put into the horse's mouth and how this small bit can enable its rider to turn about the whole body of a horse. He also makes mention of a small rudder (the ancient rudder or helm was made in the shape of an oar) that enables the pilot to steer a huge ship.

In the same sense, our tongues are very small members when compared with other members of our body yet they are able to govern the whole body. They control the direction of our lives. What we speak forth determines our destiny. If we tell ourselves that we can do something, it motivates our bodies to at least attempt it. I remember watching a man on television getting ready to bungee jump off the highest bridge in America and he kept telling himself that he could do it. Sure enough, his words propelled him a few minutes later to take that plunge.

The power of these small items is further exemplified when we consider they must also overcome contrary forces. The bit must overcome the wild nature of the horse and the rudder must fight the winds and currents that would drive the ship off course to keep both pointed in the right direction.

Our tongue must also fight against contrary forces—mainly human nature. The wild nature and fierce passions of the flesh can be brought under control when man is able to control his tongue.

The ten spies brought back a negative report and said that there was no way they could defeat the giants they saw in the land of Canaan; their words paralyzed them with such fear that they were unable to move forward with faith. If they could have controlled their tongues by not giving a negative report and instead gave a positive report like Joshua and Caleb did, their words would have created faith in God's promises and given them the courage needed to advance forward into Canaan.

In seeking to fulfill God's purpose for our lives, our human nature will try to get us off course by creating fear and doubt but our tongues can control our human nature by speaking forth a positive report of what God can do.

Although our tongues are very small members of the body, they are nonetheless very powerful. Very few words have to be spoken to change the course of events. A judge says guilty or not guilty and it affects the destiny of a person and his family for years to come. The president of the United States says a few words and the country is at war. A parent tells their child yes or no and it affects the future of that child. The fact is all it takes is a few words to start wars, a few words to end a marriage, a few words to ruin a friendship . . .

In verse 5, the writer illustrates that even though the tongue is a little member as compared with the rest of the body (as the bit and rudder are when compared to the horse and ship), it nonetheless boasts great things. Being conscious of its influence and power, it boasts largely of what it can do.

The irony of boasting is that it comes from a place of insecurity; usually people boast of things that they only wish they had done or accomplished, trying desperately to get people to believe they did something that in reality they never did. We have probably all heard the fisherman's story of how he caught a 15-pound fish but it got away or the story of the hunter who shot a 10-point buck only to have it run off.

It has been said that the man who sings his own praises always gets the wrong pitch. Nobody likes to be around someone who boasts about himself or tries to always be the center of attention.

Instead, if we use our words to boost up others, we will have many friends. People like to be around those who make them feel good about themselves.

The Fiery Effect of Words

James 3:5b-6 says, ". . . Consider what a great forest is set on fire by a small spark. The tongue also is a fire, a world of evil among the parts of the body. It corrupts the whole body, sets the whole course of one's life on fire, and is itself set on fire by hell."

Verse 5 gives the sense that a very little fire or even just a spark is capable of igniting a large quantity of combustible materials. I remember on a cold night in October many years back, the teens in my youth group were trying to get some logs to burn; all it took to get the fire going was a spark. All it takes is a spark to kindle a big pile of wood and, as we have seen, to set a forest on fire. A very little fire can very easily lead to a big fire.

In 1871, a fire that started in a barn in Chicago eventually spread over the entire city, consuming more than 2,000 acres of property and taking 250 lives. It also resulted in 100,000 people left homeless, 17,500 buildings destroyed, and $400 million in damages.

A few fiery quarrelsome words can lead to a big blaze of contention. "As charcoal to embers and as wood to fire, so is a quarrelsome person for kindling strife" (Proverbs 26:21).

For example, John tries to draw Sam into a quarrel because Sam won't agree with him on a certain issue. This irritates Sam and leads to dissension as Sam is now angry with John. But the dissension does not end there because Sam now goes to his friends and tells them how John tried to draw him into an argument and now there are many more people drawn into the dissension. What started out as a simple disagreement has now turned into a big blaze of contention. John now has not only one person mad at him but many others whom he did nothing to. This shows the combustible nature of words that are spoken in anger.

Is it not also true that a few words spoken in gossip can lead to a big blaze of speculation?

Proverbs 26:22 further says, "The words of a gossip are like choice morsels; they go down to the inmost parts."

For example, John shares with Joe some juicy information he heard about Mike and Joe, after contemplating on what he heard, then tells Michelle about it but adds a little bit to the story to whet Michelle's appetite so she will take the information in and digest it and then Michelle tells Mary but adds a little bit more to make it even tastier and by the time the story gets back to Mike, it is blown so much out of proportion that it bears little resemblance to the truth. What started out as a small matter has now become a massive fireball of speculation that could very well ruin Mike's reputation. Sometimes, the damage done by gossip can never be amended, much like the damage done by a fire.

Joseph Stowell in his book *The Weight of Your Words* writes:

> Gossip adds fuel to the fire created by the tongue. Gossips have a great ability to keep division and strife at a fever pitch by sharing bits of information that are difficult to ignore or forget. The "juicy morsels" stay with us, permanently staining our perceptions of and appreciation for those about whom we are hearing. The vicious chain of gossip continues until it finally comes up against someone willing to stop spreading information about feuding factions and start praying. Only then will the fire die down.[1]

Proverbs 26:20 states, "Without wood a fire goes out; without a gossip a quarrel dies down." So when someone comes to us with bits of information regarding someone that we are not certain of, don't entertain their speculation and add fuel to the fire; instead, walk away and the fiery strife that they attempted to create will die down.

A story is told of a gossiper who spread a malicious, untrue story about town. When confronted with the falsehood, the person was most repentant and voiced a desire to make amends. The forgiving, innocent party asked the tale bearer to do two things. First, take a bagful of feathers and deposit one on the doorstep of each home in which the lie had been left. This was done. Then, the gossiper was told to return to those steps and collect each and every feather. Needless to say, the winds had scattered the feathers and the gossiper returned to the innocent person with no feathers. The innocent person's reply was "while I forgive you gladly, do not forget that you can never undo the damage your untrue words have done." The lesson learned was truly a bitter one.

The tongue is a fire, a world of evil all in itself. Perjury, slander, obscenity, gossip, degradation, falsehood, and lying—all these evils have arisen because of the tongue. Who can measure the amount of strife, wars, alienations, suspicions, and contentions that it has produced?

Fire not only grows quickly and creates heat; it also defiles. A fire can so soil a house and its contents that everything must be destroyed because of the damage. So too can the tongue defile the whole body. There is nothing that has so great a moral influence on our whole being as our tongues. Usually acts of violence are brought on first by the agitation of words spoken in anger and marital affairs are enabled by lies. When a person allows himself to speak an evil word, it sets in motion other things that lead to evil acts.

When fire spreads, it destroys everything in its path. Our tongues can also cause much damage and even destroy when they are beset by the fire of hell. It is the devil who puts thoughts into people's minds to say evil things; he knows better than anyone the powerful influence of words to cause damage and even destroy. The devil has come to steal, kill, and destroy (John 10:10) and one way he does this is through the words of people. Many times words are spoken because of sudden impulses or thoughts that people have which they act on without thinking rationally about the origin of such evil impulses.

An Unruly Member

James 3:7-8 says, "All kinds of animals, birds, reptiles and sea creatures are being tamed and have been tamed by mankind, but no human being can tame the tongue. It is a restless evil, full of deadly poison."

In these verses, James states that there is no person who has the power to keep the tongue under control. Everything else but this has been tamed by man. We have seen the remarkable power of man to tame the wild and savage natures of animals and creatures of all kinds. It has been said that there is no kind of creature that cannot be tamed by man with proper perseverance. One of the blessings that God gave man was that he would have dominion over every living thing in the earth (Genesis 1:28).

Although man has the capacity to tame all creatures, one thing that he cannot tame is the tongue. The tongue is a restless evil that cannot be tamed by man. It is full of deadly poison that can quickly kill a relationship, paralyze love, poison minds, destroy faith, and tear down reputations.

So what can man do if he cannot tame this restless member of his body that is full of deadly poison?

The Psalmist David gives us the key to controlling the tongue. He writes, "Set a guard over my mouth, Lord; keep watch over the door of my lips. Do not let my heart be drawn to what is evil so that I take part in wicked deeds along with those who are evildoers; do not let me eat their delicacies" (Psalms 141:3-4). David knew that his heart was the key to right speech.

"For the mouth speaks what the heart is full of" (Matthew 12:34). Whatever we allow to come into our hearts will eventually come out through our mouths. When we fill our hearts with things that are lovely, that are morally right, that are pure, then these are the kinds of things that will come out of our mouths. When we read and meditate on God's word, we fill our hearts with God's precepts and this is what we will want to talk about. When Jesus is the Lord of the heart, then He will be the Lord of the lips also. Whatever is in the well of the heart is what will be drawn out with the bucket of the mouth.

Before I gave my heart to Christ, I quite frequently spoke vulgar words because I was putting vulgar things into my heart. Every day I was either reading smut magazines or watching R-rated movies. I put garbage in and it was garbage that came out. After I accepted Christ into my heart, however, I no longer had a desire to digest such vulgar things but instead I started reading the Bible every day, sometimes for hours at a time. I just couldn't seem to get enough of God's word. I also read other religious books that built my faith and knowledge in the things of God. So when I was around others, this is what came out of my mouth. A friend of mine told me that he didn't want to be around me anymore because the only thing that I ever wanted to talk about was the Bible and God. I received that as a compliment because it meant that my heart was right.

A Double Standard

James 3:9-12 says, "With the tongue we praise our Lord and Father, and with it we curse human beings, who have been made in God's likeness. Out of the same mouth come praise and cursing. My brothers and sisters, this should not be. Can both fresh water and salt water flow from the same spring? My brothers and sisters, can a fig tree bear olives, or a grapevine bear figs? Neither can a salt spring produce fresh water."

The writer here points to the absurdity of blessing one who has to us the relation of a Father and then cursing those who are made in his likeness. They praise and worship God out of their mouths but yet out of those same mouths they curse men. Thus, out of the same mouth come two opposite things.

For example, a person goes to church on Sunday morning and worships God with his mouth but then after church, goes home and slanders the pastor and his message in front of his family. Out of the same mouth came praise to God but also cursing of someone made after God's image.

The writer exclaims "this should not be."

In verse 11, the writer continues on with this double standard way. Does fresh water and salt water both flow out of the same spring? Such things do not occur in the works of nature, and they should not be found in man.

Water that comes out of a fountain is to be life-giving and our words are to give life also. "The mouth of the righteous is a fountain of life . . ." (Proverbs 10:11). If we were to open our mouths wide to drink of the water coming out of a fountain, we would be surprised (and probably disappointed too) if the water was salty, as only fresh water is supposed to come out of a fountain.

In verse 12, the writer asks, "can a fig tree bear olives or a grapevine bear figs?" Such a thing is impossible in nature because nature reproduces after its kind. A fig-tree bears only figs, an olive tree bears only olives, and a grapevine only bears grapes.

Thus, those who bless and then curse people with their words are setting a double-standard with their mouth. They are not consistent in what they say and they will soon lose the respect and trust of those who know them.

The fact is our tongues do not need to be a double-standard – they do have the capacity to consistently be a blessing.

Warren Wiersbe, author of the popular "BE" series of Bible commentaries, writes in his "BE Mature" commentary on the book of James:

The power of speech is one of the greatest powers God has given us. With the tongue, man can praise God, pray, preach the Word, and lead the lost to Christ. What a privilege! But with that same tongue he can tell lies that could ruin a man's reputation or break a person's heart. The ability to speak words is the ability to influence others and accomplish tremendous tasks, and yet we take this ability for granted.[2]

In this first chapter, we examined more of the negative influences of words on ourselves and others. But in the remainder of this book, we will examine more of the positive influence of words on ourselves and others when we allow what we say to come under God's influence.

Challenge Questions:

1) What is one way that you can control your tongue so that you can fulfill God's will for my life?
2) When you are around others, do you find it easier to talk more about your own interests or about the interests of others? Why would it be more beneficial to focus more on the interests of others?
3) When someone comes to you with some juicy information about someone else, how would you respond? Would you stay and entertain the gossip or walk away? By choosing to walk away, what effect would this have on the gossip?
4) How consistent are you with your words? Do you speak the same things outside of church that you speak in church? What are the results of one who is not consistent with their words?

Chapter 2

LIVING WORRY-FREE

Philippians 4:6-7

I F SOMEONE TELLS YOU THAT they never worry about things, they are probably deceiving you and themselves. Anxiety is a common human emotion that we all experience from time to time. As a matter of fact, a moderate amount of anxiety can be helpful at times. It helps us to avoid dangerous situations and increases our alertness. It's over-anxiety that prevents us from functioning properly.

So it is not a matter of never having anxiety as much as it is finding a way to not let the anxiety grow to the point that it takes control of our lives. This is what we mean by worry-free living.

We all have weaknesses and worry has always been one of mine. It has been a constant struggle for me to not allow worry to control my life. But as I have been applying the principles found in this book to my own life, I have found one of the keys to keep worry contained in my life is giving thanks to God each day. This is what I want to share with you in this chapter—How worry-free living comes from thanksgiving.

The Negative Effects of Worry

Philippians 4:6a—"Do not be anxious about anything . . ."

In verse 6, Paul instructs the saints at Philippi to stop worrying so much. Apparently, there were situations there in the church that was causing this. Perhaps, the dispute between Euodias and Synteche was causing division and this became a source of worry. Also, the Christians during this time were being severely persecuted.

Worry is a reaction to an unfamiliar threat that originates inside the mind. It's a perception of something that may or may not happen. The fact is most things that people worry about never do come to pass but are merely figments of their imaginations although to them they seem real. I have looked back many times on things that I worried about in my own life that never did come to pass and realized the waste of time and focus that it had cost me.

John McClure writes:

> Unpleasant experiences in life which produce anxiety are threats to one or more physical, emotional, or spiritual needs. Crime, war, violent weather, and illness threaten our physical well-being and cause us to be anxious. There are also those experiences which in reality do not threaten our physical well-being but we perceive them to be threatening. For example many people are afraid of all snakes, even though many snakes are harmless. Actually, it is not our experiences that produce anxiety; it is what we believe and are telling ourselves about our experiences that are the sources of anxiety.[1]

Worry has been described as a rocking chair, it will give you something to do, but it won't get you anywhere. It has also been described as interest paid on trouble before it is due.

What are some of the effects of worry? It causes one to have sleepless nights and paralyzing thoughts and feelings of what might be. It controls one's thinking and actions. It leads to stress, which causes physical and emotional illnesses such as ulcers and depression. It causes some to overeat and others to not eat enough. With some it may cause problems with speaking such as stuttering. It has a tendency to cause people to isolate themselves from others. Worst of all, worry is a peace robber as it causes inner turmoil and confusion, and thus a lack of peace. When we spend our days worrying about things that are in the future, it robs us of the present day joy that God wants us to live in.

When we allow ourselves to have negative perceptions of the future, it will inevitably lead to negative expressions as well. Isn't it true that the words we speak are affected first by the thoughts we think. Worrisome thoughts will inevitably lead to negative expressions such as complaining about what we have or do not have. "If I had a better job, I wouldn't be struggling to make ends meet." "If I just had a bigger house, it would be easier for me to have a place to work out so I could lose weight and get in shape." The negative perception of the ten spies as being as grasshoppers in comparison to the inhabitants of Canaan led to negative expressions such as complaining that they were not able to possess the land of Canaan because the inhabitants were too strong for them and the cities were walled. Their negative perception led to worry that stifled their faith and led to negative words, which created even more fear.

When we speak forth negative words over things that we are worrying about, it stifles our faith even more and makes our perceptions of the future even more negative and overwhelming. We allow fear and worry to become an even greater stronghold in our lives when we speak it forth. Is it any wonder that Paul exhorted the saints in the church at Philippi to stop their worrying?

Overcoming Worry through Thanksgiving

Philippians 4:6b—". . . but in every situation, by prayer and petition, with thanksgiving, present your requests to God."

One spiritual remedy that Paul gives here to overcome worry is through prayer. Paul writes "but in every situation, by prayer . . ."

We are to bring all of our worries to God in prayer—big ones as well as small ones, for even the small worries will turn out to be big worries if we don't deal with them.

The whole concept of prayer is for us to be willing to let go of those things that trouble us and to seek the vertical plane with God where we can allow Him to take full control of our situations. Prayer gives us a way to release our burdens and worries to God. "Cast all your anxiety on him because he cares for you" (I Peter 5:7).

It's so easy to repress worry which just creates more anxiety in our lives. But through prayer, we can open our hearts to God and express to Him our struggles and weaknesses such as worry.

"For we do not have a high priest who is unable to empathize with our weaknesses, but we have one who has been tempted in every way, just as we are—yet he did not sin. Let us then approach God's throne of grace with confidence, so that we may receive mercy and find grace to help us in our time of need" (Hebrews 4:15-16).

God will listen when we speak to him; all He asks is that we come to Him and be honest with what we are struggling with. Although God already knows that we may be struggling with worry, He still takes pleasure when we show our confidence and trust in Him by expressing it. Thus, our words of sincerity to God influence Him to act on our behalf by providing us with mercy and grace in our time of need.

A second remedy that Paul gives us to overcome worry is through words of thanksgiving. When we first release our worries to God through the avenue of prayer, it enables us then to offer words of thanksgiving to God, which enable us to overcome worry.

First, words of thanksgiving produce an appreciation for what we do have. Most things that people worry about are things that they have no control over and that involve temporal things. We worry about whether we will get that job promotion, or about the gain on our investments, or about whether our house will sell if we put it on the market. When we worry over things that we have no control over, it causes us to lose sight of the other things in our lives that we have to be really thankful for.

However, when we speak forth words of thanksgiving, it produces an awareness and appreciation for what we do have. It reminds us of the good things that God has done and is doing in our lives. "Praise the Lord, my soul, and forget not all his benefits" (Ps. 103:2). We realize that there are more important things to give our attention to instead of worrying all the time over things that are beyond our control. We become thankful for even the little things in our lives and content with what we do have.

You see it's not in what we have or do not have that enables us to be thankful to God and happy, but rather learning to be content with what God has already given us. Contentment is not the fulfillment of what we want, but rather the realization of what we have. Paul wrote, "I am not saying this because I am in need, for I have learned to be content whatever the circumstances" (Philippians 4:11). When we are thankful for the things that really count in our lives, then the other things that are beyond our control become less important. But to realize what we have requires us at times to speak words of thanksgiving so we can remind ourselves of those things.

After I had served as a pastor to a church for six years and decided to move on, I did not have another pastorate to go to right away. So I moved back to my home town of Beloit, Wisconsin with my wife and four-year-old daughter until I could find another pastorate. At my church that I had left, we had lived in a spacious five-bedroom parsonage that had its own master bath; but in Beloit we moved into a small two-bedroom apartment that to say the least was very cramped.

To make matters worse, I was not doing the thing that I loved the most, serving as a pastor; instead, I was working on an assembly line putting items into a cardboard box and standing on a hard concrete floor for 12-hour shifts.

Because of my living and work conditions, I found myself complaining every day and wondering why I had ever moved to Beloit. I was not very happy during that time and my wife and daughter both knew it because they were the ones who heard the grumbling and complaining every day.

One day, as I was sitting around and feeling sorry for myself, the thought came to me that I did have much to be thankful for. At least we had a roof over our heads that kept us dry and warm. At least I had a job that provided money for us to buy food. At least I had a reliable vehicle that got me back and forth to work.

God was really trying to teach me during this time to be content and thankful for what I did have because although it may not have been what I wanted for myself at that time, it was what God had provided to me for that time.

So every day instead of grumbling and complaining, I began to give God thanks for my small apartment, for my vehicle, for my job. By doing so, I was able to remind myself of what I did have and this realization produced an appreciation in my heart for those things.

Our apartment then became bigger and more spacious to me (at least in my mind) and my job became more satisfying.

Second, words of thanksgiving produce a renewal of our faith for the present. Worry will paralyze our faith like nothing else will. We doubt whether our situations will ever improve and whether God will ever answer our prayers. The pressures and obstacles of life appear greater than God's promises. We can't pray with the belief that God will answer. We find ourselves confessing what God isn't doing instead of what we believe He can and will do.

However, when we speak forth words of thanksgiving, it produces a renewal of faith for the present. We take on a clearer view of God in our present affairs by remembering the past wonders of God in our lives. We realize that God is faithful and what He did before for us, He can do again. It lifts our faith up in God's greatness to a higher level and we realize again that He is indeed greater than any obstacles we may be facing. In our renewed faith, we begin to confess what we believe God is going to do in our circumstances. We are able to approach God with new boldness and assurance.

Thus, we are able to let go of the worry since there is a renewed awareness that almighty God is in control of our lives and situations. The renewal of faith drives away worry because worry and faith cannot coexist—worry cannot remain in an atmosphere where faith has been created.

Terry Law writes from his book on *The Power of Praise and Worship*:

> Thanksgiving has a way of getting the wheels of faith moving in our spirit. There is a certain amount of inertia in our faith that has to be overcome. Thanksgiving is action that we can take against that inertia to get our faith active. When we begin to recount what God has done, it doesn't

take very long to get excited about what He is about to do now. Thanksgiving helps us to focus not on the problem, but on the answer. It reminds us that we are really victors when we are exalting God. The Devil will try to hold our minds by having us focus on the reality of the present. He will encourage us to think thoughts full of fear, but thanksgiving turns that whole process around and gets us moving in God's direction. I have noticed this principle over the years in the preaching of many men that God is using.[2]

When my daughter was stricken with spinal meningitis, the doctors gave her a 50% chance of surviving. She was four years old at the time and as I sat in the waiting room, fear gripped my heart and I was overcome with worry that I would never be able to take her to the park again or hear her laugh again.

But then my wife reminded me of what God had done before for Brianna. Just a few months previously, she had been involved in a serious accident and almost died, but God miraculously healed her. We believed then that God would heal her, my wife reminded me, and what God did before, He could do again.

As I began to reflect on how quickly Brianna had recovered from that previous injury despite the negative reports of the doctors, it gave me faith for the present. This enabled me to begin to confess what I believed God could now do for her. And as I continued to give thanks to God for her healing, my faith continued to grow and the paralyzing fear that had literally overwhelmed me just a short time before was replaced with a peace and confidence that God was in control. And then just a few hours after this, the doctor came into the waiting room and gave us the good news that Brianna was going to make a full recovery.

Third, words of thanksgiving produce a perspective that every situation that God allows in our lives has a good purpose. When we are in the midst of difficult circumstances and feeling overwhelmed with worry, it can be very difficult to see any good in what is happening. All we see is the present reality of what is happening and that things are not getting any better. We begin to imagine the worst scenarios of what can happen and we find ourselves bound with even more worry.

However, when we speak forth words of thanksgiving, it produces a perspective that every situation in our lives has a good purpose. We find ourselves thanking God for the very things that He allowed in our lives that before were so overwhelming to bear. Instead of praying for constant deliverance, we pray for God's purpose to be fulfilled through the circumstances. With a clearer perspective, we are able to see the good things that God is bringing out of our situations and the spiritual graces and fruit that He is developing within us.

I believe in every situation that God allows in our lives that there is some good purpose we can find to be thankful for. I Thessalonians 5:18 says, "Give thanks in all circumstances; for this is God's will for you in Christ Jesus." Notice the word "in." We are not commanded to give thanks for everything that happens but rather we are to give thanks in the midst of whatever is happening in our lives. The fact is not everything that happens in our lives is the will of God but rather whatever God allows in our lives is what we are to give God thanks for. However, in our human nature, it is easier to give God thanks when we are on the mountain top than in the valley; it is easier for us to give God thanks in prosperity than in want; it is easier for us to give God thanks in health than in sickness. Yet this scripture says that we are to give God thanks IN EVERYTHING—in whatever God allows in our lives. This can be a great challenge at times but yet possible through taking on a proper perspective of things.

H.W. Beecher states well how the thankful can pick up like a magnet the goodness of God. "If one should give me a dish of sand, and tell me there were particles of iron in it, I might look for them with my eyes, and search for them with my clumsy fingers, and be unable to detect them; but let me take a magnet, and sweep through it, and it would draw to itself the almost invisible particles by the mere power of attraction. The unthankful heart, like my finger in the sand, discovers no mercies, but let a thankful heart sweep through the day, and as the magnet finds the iron, so it will find, in every hour, some heavenly blessing, only the iron in God's sand is gold."

It's how we view things that make all the difference in what our attitude will be and in what we say. Thanksgiving comes from the Anglo-Saxon word "thinkful." As we think and meditate on God's blessings in our lives and are made more aware of those blessings, there is an attitude of gratitude that will then seek for vocal expression. This gratitude involves such a deep level of appreciation in what God has done for us that the overflowing joy that has been welled up in our hearts springs forth into spontaneous and joyful expressions of thanks. The bible says that we speak forth what is in our hearts. Thus, the giving of thanks is an outward expression of our inner feelings of joy and gratitude. Even the prayer over our meals should come from a heart of gratitude over what God has provided us to eat.

In the story of the ten lepers, only one of the ten returned to give thanks for their healing because only he took the time to think about the course of events that led to his healing and who the source of that healing was. The other lepers' sole focus was getting to the priest to be declared clean by him so they could become a part of society again. The Samaritan, however, had a deeper level of appreciation of what had happened and turned back to give thanks to the author of his cure, who he wished to have the glory of it, before he received the benefit of it. The Samaritan's gratitude for his healing created an overflowing joy that welled up in his heart that could not be confined and with a loud voice, he glorified Christ. His words of thanksgiving to Christ came naturally and spontaneously as he first took the time to meditate on the blessing and who the source of that blessing was. Jesus distinguished him from the other nine lepers, as it was by his faith that he was made whole.

Peace Instead of Worry

Philippians 4:7, "And the peace of God, which transcends all understanding, will guard your hearts and your minds in Christ Jesus."

One definition of peace is the calm, quiet, and order that take place in the justified soul. It is the contentment of a right relationship with God and the calm assurance that God is watching over one's life.

Man seeks to gain peace by logical understanding. God's peace, however, transcends all human understanding. This peace of God is so vast that man's mind can never understand it or find it or produce it. It is beyond all human finite understanding for it is a peace that comes from God.

There is a song that we sing in church sometimes entitled *Wonderful Peace* that expresses this well:

> Peace! Peace! Wonderful peace.
> Coming down from the Father above;
> Sweep over my spirit forever I pray
> In fathomless billows of love.

God's peace will guard our hearts and minds from the intrusion of anxiety just as a camp or castle is guarded from the intrusion of the enemy.

Our minds and hearts are preserved in peace through Christ Jesus. This occurs when we take our focus off of our trying circumstances and focus instead on Jesus. Speaking forth words of thanksgiving produces in us a thorough confidence and trust in Christ—that He is indeed greater than all our circumstances, He is in control of every aspect of our lives even though all may seem hopeless, and He is aware of everything in our lives and is working out His perfect will for us. It's through such confidence and trust in Christ that we can maintain perfect peace. Isaiah 26:3 states, "You will keep in perfect peace those whose minds are steadfast, because they trust in you." Such perfect trust in Christ prevents worry from intruding back into our minds.

There is a reading that reminds me to not worry about things that I cannot control because God is in control. It says, "Good morning. This is God! I will be handling all your problems today. I will not need your help, so have a good day."

One day, a friend of mine called me and asked if I would like to go for a ride in an airplane. I had not been up in a plane for many years but this sounded fun so I said okay. As we ascended up in the little two-seater plane, everything down below seemed so small and the cars looked like they were moving in slow motion. I felt safe up there, especially knowing that my friend who was piloting that little plane was a jet captain by trade.

We were trying to locate my home church and when my pilot friend spotted it; he asked me if I had spotted it, to which I responded in the negative. So he decided to do a quick loop so I could get another look and hopefully spot the church. Well, when he did the quick loop, he failed to inform me that you never want to focus on an object in the midst of the loop because it can cause you to get sick to your stomach, very dizzy, and, yes, very loopy.

After doing the quick loop, he asked me again if I could spot the church and I was able to see it but the problem was I was now seeing two churches side by side.

By this time, my stomach was churning and I had all but forgotten that my life was in the hands of a very capable pilot; I really believed I was going to die up there. I told my friend to get me back to the airport as quickly as possible as I started to hyperventilate with fear and anxiety.

I have thought about that incident many times and realized that is what we do in life sometimes. We try to focus too much on things when there are sudden twists and turns in our lives and in our attempts to figure things out we end up confused and fearful of what is going to happen when all along Jesus is piloting our lives. All He wants us to do is to just sit back and enjoy the ride realizing that we are in the hands of a very capable pilot and so there is no need to worry about things that we have no control over anyways.

A hymn entitled "Calm" by Horatius Bonar, 1808-1889, reads,

I stand upon the Mount of God
  With sunlight in my soul;
I hear the storms in vales beneath,
  I hear the thunders roll.
But I am calm with Thee, my God,
  Beneath these glorious skies;
And to the height on which I stand,
  No storms, nor clouds, can rise.
O this is life! O this is joy!
  My God, to find Thee so;
Thy face to see, Thy voice to hear,
  And all Thy love to know.

So in summary, let's not allow worry to control our lives to the point that we can't enjoy the present day God has given us. Life is too short to worry about things in the future that most of the time we have no control over anyway. Let's release our worry and live worry—free by giving thanks to God each day and reminding ourselves of the things that God has provided for us and things that God has done. Yes, it works! The key to worry-free living is thanksgiving. Our words have a positive influence on us when they are words of thanksgiving.

Challenge Questions:

1) Have you ever noticed that most things you worry about never come to pass but are figments of your imagination? But the effects of worry are real. What are some of the effects of worry?

2) How do you usually begin your day—with complaining or thanksgiving? How would beginning your day with thanksgiving help you to live worry-free?

3) We are to give God thanks in everything according to the scriptures. How can you make this a reality in your life?

4) Through whom can you preserve your heart and mind in peace? Explain why this is true.

Chapter 3

WHEN YOU'RE OFFENDED

Luke 17:3-6

I N VERSE 1, JESUS SAYS "Things that cause people to stumble are bound to come . . ." The "things" that Jesus was referring to can include many different things but more specifically he was referring to offenses as we shall see in the verses that follow. Somebody does or says something that offends us and it could very easily cause us to stumble in a spiritual sense by making us angry and bitter. As long as we are involved in relationships with others, there is always the possibility that something will be said or done that could offend us or that we may take the wrong way.

We interact with people daily at home, at work, at play, and at church. The relationships we form with people are sometimes casual while other relationships are more intimate, such as the relationships we have with close friends and family members. In each of these daily interactions with others and in all relationships, there is potential for misunderstandings, for disagreements, and for conflicts. But it is those whose relationships we value the most who have the ability to hurt us the most. This is true because we expect more from them.

In the New Testament, offense is often described as an entrapment used by the enemy. Offense is the trap that Satan uses to cause believers to stumble. It seems to come out of nowhere and blind sides us when we least expect it.

In this chapter, we will show how one can avoid stumbling over the trap of offense when they have been offended.

So it is not a matter as to whether offenses will come our way as much as it is about what our response will be when they do come. How we respond determines if we stumble over the trap of offense.

Seeking Forgiveness through Reconciliation

In Luke 17:3-4, Jesus states, "So watch yourselves. If your brother or sister sins against you, rebuke them; and if they repent, forgive them. Even if they sin against you seven times in a day and seven times come back to you saying 'I repent,' you must forgive them."

Jesus tells his disciples to watch out, to be on guard. He tells them this because, as verse one says things that cause us to stumble such as offenses will come, and there was a certain way that they should respond when they were offended. The same applies to us today.

Jesus then tells them what their response should be when they were offended.

First of all, when someone offends them, they should go to the offender and relate the matter of the offense with the hope that the offender might acknowledge his wrong and repent.

"If your brother or sister sins, go and point out their fault, just between the two of you. If they listen to you, you have won them over" (Matt. 18:15).

When the matter of the offense is shared in a spirit of meekness with the motivation being reconciliation, our words can have a powerful influence in resolving the matter.

Sometimes, the offenders might not even be aware that they have offended us and as we share the matter of the offense, it gives them the opportunity to explain what they meant. It might have been a simple misunderstanding that can be easily cleared up.

It could also be that the offenders are already feeling guilty about what they might have said or did to upset us; by us going to them and sharing the matter of the offense, it gives them the opportunity to repent.

Also, by sharing the matter of the offense, our words can also have a powerful influence on us as it gives us the opportunity to release some the hurt that we may be feeling with the very one who offended us.

Many times, however, people will go to other people to speak about their offenses in an attempt to get them to validate their hurts and grudges, but such speaking just makes the hurt even deeper. It can also make those with whom they share their hurt angry at the offender as well, even though the offender has done nothing personally to offend them.

How much better it is to go directly to the one who has offended us and allow our words to bring reconciliation.

Some may feel, however, that it should be the offenders who should take the initiative in reconciliation since they are the one in the wrong. Jesus says, however, that as believers, we are to take the initiative in reconciliation. After all, we wronged God yet He initiated the reconciliation by sending His Son to reconcile us to Himself.

"All this is from God, who reconciled us to himself through Christ and gave us the ministry of reconciliation" (II Corinthians 5:18).

Second, Jesus tells His disciples to not only go to their offender and relate the matter of the offense, but be willing also to forgive if their offender repents of his wrongdoing.

Sometimes, people will continue to hold resentment even after their offender apologizes as a means of making him suffer longer, but notice that Jesus makes no exception and says we must forgive our offenders if they repent. If we fail to forgive them after they repent, then we are denying the very power that our words had to bring about reconciliation.

Third, Jesus tells His disciples that if they are offended seven times in one day and seven times their offender repents of his wrongdoing, they must still forgive.

Seven is the number of divine completion in the Bible. Thus, Jesus was telling His disciples that their forgiveness had to be unconditional and that no matter how many times they were offended by someone, they still needed to forgive. They were to maintain an attitude that was always ready to help and forgive the offender.

Jesus' statement concerning forgiving seven times in a day, however, is not meant to encourage and condone habitual sin. Nor is He saying that the believer must allow someone to severely mistreat or abuse him or her indefinitely.

Forgiveness—A Choice One Makes

Luke 17:5, "The apostles said to the Lord, 'Increase our faith!'"

When Jesus talks about forgiving others, the first thing the disciples say is, "Lord, give us more faith." They realized that they did not have the power or ability within themselves to forgive in such measure and they needed more faith to do so.

You see, we have a need to forgive by faith. Forgiveness is of divine origin and therefore it's impossible for us to forgive others in our own strength and ability.

Forgiveness is not a feeling but is an act of the will on our part. It is a choice that we make—a choice that we make even when we don't feel like it. This is why we must forgive by faith.

H. Norman Wright, who has written many popular books on marriage, writes concerning this truth of forgiveness being a choice we make:

> It is a clear and logical action on your part. It is not a
> soothing, comforting, overwhelming emotional response
> that erases the fact from your memory.[1]

Colossians 3:12-13 exhorts us to put on as God's elect people spiritual graces such as forgiving one another, "Therefore, as God's chosen people, holy and dearly loved, clothe yourselves with compassion, kindness, humility, gentleness and patience. Bear with each other and forgive one another if any of you has a grievance against someone. Forgive as the Lord forgave you."

When I get ready each morning and put on my clothes for the day, I don't go to my wife and always ask her what I should wear (although there have been some days that I wished I had asked for her advice); I make the choice myself. Nobody else has to make that choice for me.

The same applies when forgiving others. When we "put on" or clothe ourselves with forgiveness, we make the choice to do so; no one else can make that choice for us. That piece of clothing may not look right at first and may appear to not fit right, but we put it on anyway.

The reason we make that choice to forgive others is because Christ has forgiven us. When we compare how much we were forgiven of

God, the hurts and insults that we must forgive others of is small in comparison.

Making such a choice to forgive goes contrary to all human and carnal reasoning. But we have been transformed through the power of God. So we can choose to forgive, or we can choose to hold a grudge. God never takes the choice away from us to choose right or wrong. But we do have the power through God to make the right choice—that of forgiving. God would not command us to forgive and not give us the power to do so.

Our flesh and feelings will always try to convince us that we have a right to hold onto a grudge or to harbor ill-will toward our offender. However, when we make the choice to forgive our offender by faith, we decide to no longer allow our will to be directed by how we feel or perceive things to be.

This is why some Christians never forgive because they haven't realized that it begins with a choice that they must make even though they may have deep hurts yet. It requires a step of faith on their part. They keep waiting for their hurts to heal first but the irony is the deep hurts one has will not begin to heal until they first make the choice to forgive.

There is a true story told of Corrie Ten Boom that illustrates this point. After suffering the horrors of a Nazi concentration camp during World War II, Corrie was finally released from prison. Her sister had died in that terrible prison. Her father and brother had also been put to death in German prisons. It was only a miracle that Corrie survived.

After the war, Corrie traveled through Europe, telling how God's grace had helped her forgive, and how God could bring healing to all those lives had been torn apart by war.

One night, after speaking in a church service, Corrie found herself face to face with a man who had been a guard at the concentration camp where Corrie had been imprisoned. He had been so cruel, seeming to enjoy every act of persecution carried out against the helpless prisoners. How could he even think of speaking to her?

He told Corrie how God had washed away his sins and his radiant face and joyous words gave witness to God's saving grace in his life. Then, he held out his hand to Corrie. As he did, all the old hurt had come back to her in an instant.

She could not move her arm – she could not force her hand to take his outstretched hand. She silently prayed to God—she could not forgive him and take his hand in her own strength; she needed His help to forgive him. She then simply made the decision to forgive him through faith and instantly she felt a genuine, forgiving spirit in her heart as she slowly raised her hand to take the hand of her former tormentor.

Uprooting Bitterness through Our Words

Luke 17:6 says, "If you have faith as small as a mustard seed, you can say to this mulberry tree, 'Be uprooted and planted in the sea,' and it will obey you."

Usually, when someone offends us and we don't deal with the offense immediately, the offense leads to anger which, when allowed to linger, can turn to bitterness.

In verse 6, the root of bitterness can be compared to a mulberry tree. The mulberry tree was known for its enormous roots, as thick, as numerous, and as wide spread into the deep soil below as the branches extend into the air above. Bitterness when allowed to linger in the soil of one's heart will spread its deadly roots deeper and further into one's heart resulting in their heart becoming poisoned. A poisoned heart then produces poisoned fruit.

Joel Osteen, Pastor of America's biggest church and best-selling author, writes concerning this internal root of bitterness that affects every area of our lives:

> The Scripture says, "Make sure that no root of bitterness shoots forth and causes trouble and many become contaminated by it." Notice, bitterness is described as a root. Think about that. You can't see a root; it's deep down under the ground. But you can be sure of this: A bitter root will produce bitter fruit. If we have bitterness on the inside, it's going to affect every area of our lives.[2]

So when one makes the choice to forgive, what do they do next if bitterness has become rooted deep in their hearts? How do they uproot such deep-seated bitterness that is affecting every area of their life?

Jesus tells his disciples that if they had faith as small as a mustard seed, they might say to the mulberry tree to be uprooted and planted in the sea and it would obey them. Now keep in the mind that the mustard seed was the smallest of all seeds so Jesus is telling them that just the smallest amount of faith that is spoken forth out of their mouths has the power to uproot the biggest obstacle such as bitterness.

Such faith-filled words that have the power to uproot bitterness may sound like "Bitterness you're not going to stand in my way and hinder me any longer;" "Bitterness, I command you by the name of Jesus Christ to be plucked up by the roots out of my heart and thrown into the sea of forgetfulness;" "I will no longer allow bitterness to ruin my life, but I choose today to have victory."

When it comes to uprooting bitterness out of our hearts, we cannot be passive about it. As Jesus pointed out here we must speak to the mulberry tree of bitterness directly and with authority and command it to be uprooted out of our lives and planted into the sea of forgetfulness where it no longer controls us.

Once we make the decision to forgive and speak forth words of authority to bitterness, the obstacle of bitterness must obey and be rooted out of our hearts because now we allow God's supernatural power to work on our behalf, helping us to overcome a rooty issue that we never could have pulled up in our own strength.

When we speak forth words of authority to bitterness, we create an atmosphere of faith that allows God to do the supernatural. It doesn't matter how deep or widespread the roots of bitterness may be or how long those roots have been there, God's power is greater. God is able to go right to the very roots of our struggles and pull them up by the roots.

Be prepared though because even though we command the root of bitterness to be uprooted out of our hearts and it must obey our words of authority, God will usually have us still go to our offenders to totally set the record straight.

However, where before we could not even face our offenders, we now have the grace to do so because of God's own grace in our lives that enabled us to forgive. Our offenders may be shocked at first as we approach them in such a forgiving spirit but they probably also will come to be ashamed for the wrong that they did to us.

Going to those who have offended us with a meek and humble spirit and seeking to reconcile with them will complete God's work of forgiveness in us. This is usually the final step that God requires of us in this act of forgiveness.

Although forgiving those who have offended us may not take all the hurt away or erase the memories of what happened, forgiving our offenders has many wonderful benefits.

It allows our hurts to begin to heal.

It frees us from anger and guilt.

It frees us to trust people again and thus develop loving relationships with others.

It frees us to be ourselves again.

It frees us to pray and worship God with a clear conscience. "Therefore I tell you, whatever you ask for in prayer, believe that you have received it, and it will be yours. And when you stand praying, if you hold anything against anyone, forgive them, so that your Father in heaven may forgive you your sins" (Mark 11:24-25).

Probably the most important benefit is that it allows God to forgive us. You see, we do not have the freedom to ask God to forgive us if we have not forgiven others. "For if you forgive other people when they sin against you, your heavenly Father will also forgive you. But if you do not forgive others their sins, your Father will not forgive your sins" (Matthew 6:14-15). Forgiveness cannot flow toward you until it flows from you.

There was a time in my own life when I was overcome with feelings of resentment and bitterness. I had recommitted my life back to Christ and was faithfully serving in a position at a church when someone whom I looked up to and had the utmost respect for told me that I was not doing a very good job in my position. Their comment shocked me and didn't make any sense to me since I felt that I was doing a good job and I was seeing results. I felt that this person had made remarks to me that were unwarranted and unfair and I allowed those words of rebuke to bring anger and resentment into my heart.

As I allowed the anger to linger, I could sense that bitterness was creeping into my heart and putting its deadly roots deep into my heart. When I went to church, I would avoid my offender but even worse I felt the bitterness in my heart had put a rift in my relationship with God. I no longer had the freedom to worship and pray to God like I once had.

I kept trying to convince myself that I had every right to hold onto the hurt and grudge since I was the one who had been wronged. This was my way of getting back at my offender but what I didn't realize at the time that the person I was really hurting was myself.

After weeks of inner torment, I finally made up of my mind to forgive by faith. It wasn't easy, as my flesh did not yield easily. With a loud voice I commanded the root of bitterness to be uprooted from my heart for it no longer had authority to remain there. I proclaimed that whom the Son has set free is free indeed.

At that very moment, I felt God's peace come back into my heart and God's healing as it began to soothe the hurt that I had been carrying for several weeks.

That Sunday, I could not wait to get to church and meet and try to reconcile with my offender. This experience showed me how our words can influence people to become offended but also how our words can influence us to forgive those who have offended us.

So the choice is ours. When someone has done or said something to offend us, our response to the offense will determine our destiny and whether we stumble. Jesus said offenses would come but we don't have to stumble because of them. We can make the choice to forgive and when we do, reconciling with those who have offended us will become easier. Our words do have the power to influence and resolve matters with our offenders; let's allow our words to work for us, not against us.

Challenge Questions:

1) What did Jesus tell us we should do when someone has offended us? Why is this so difficult for us to do?
2) Why does your forgiveness involve a choice that you must make?
3) Why is it true that you cannot be passive when uprooting bitterness through your words?
4) What are some of the wonderful benefits that you will experience from choosing to forgive your offender?
5) Do you need to forgive someone today? If so, what steps will you take to reconcile with them?

Chapter 4

PERCEPTION THAT LEADS TO POSSESSION

Numbers 13:25-14:4

THE HUMAN BODY HAS FASCINATED scientists for thousands of years; it is made up of trillions of cells that continually grow, divide, and then die. Most people have healthy cells that properly function their entire life. Others are not as fortunate, carrying cancerous cells. Cancer begins when a dysfunctional cell grows at an accelerated rate and does not stop dividing. For some, this is fatal, while for others, brings much pain and suffering. Reckless negative words spread like cancer, literally destroying an individual, family, organization, or even an entire nation. In this chapter, we will learn about the importance of choosing our words wisely.

How many of us, after saying something, will have to ask ourselves—Did I just say that? But it is too late, the words have already gone forth and we may never be able to get those words back because the damage they caused is irreparable. We have inserted our foot into our mouth and we know it. This is why it is so vital that we be careful with the words we speak.

The words we speak influence us and others more than we realize sometimes whether for good or for bad. They can lift up or they can tear down. Words shape you and those around you. What a powerful influence words carry!

Proverbs 18:21 says, "The tongue has the power of life and death." The words we speak can either bring life to a vision or death to vision, they can create a positive environment or a negative environment, and they can motivate people to do the right thing or discourage people from doing the right thing. But as we shall see in this chapter it is our perspective that will determine whether our words are positive or negative and lead us into possession.

Examining the Source of Our Words

Numbers 13:25-31: "At the end of forty days they returned from exploring the land. They came back to Moses and Aaron and the whole Israelite community at Kadesh in the Desert of Paran. There they reported to them and to the whole assembly and showed them the fruit of the land. They gave Moses this account: 'We went into the land to which you sent us, and it does flow with milk and honey! Here is its fruit. But the people who live there are powerful and the cities are fortified and very large. We even saw descendants of Anak there. The Amalekites live in the Negev; the Hittites, Jebusites and Amorites live in the hill country; and the Canaanites live near the sea and along the Jordan.' Then Caleb silenced the people before Moses and said, 'We should go up and take possession of the land, for we can certainly do it.' But the men who had gone up with him said, 'We can't attack those people; they are stronger than we are.'"

After exploring the land of Canaan for forty days, the twelve spies returned to the congregation of Israel to share their report of what they had seen. Forty days would have given them adequate time to search out the land and to come back with a good battle strategy as they sought to possess the land. This was really their main purpose for going into Canaan and exploring the land and its peoples.

However, when they came to Moses, Aaron, and the congregation of Israel, their report was not based on a battle strategy to possess the land of Canaan. Their report started out good as they showed the fruit of the land and that surely it was a land of plenty (flowing with milk and honey). Their initial report confirmed exactly what God had told them concerning the land (Exodus 33:3). God also promised them that as they stepped into the land of Canaan, He would send an angel before them to drive out the inhabitants there (Exodus 33:2). So the fact that they saw that it was a land that was plentiful should have bolstered their faith in God's truthfulness and that He would also be true to His word to drive out the inhabitants of the land of Canaan as they went to possess it.

Although their report started out positively, it quickly went into a negative mode as we see by the word "But" in verse 28. But, they said, the people who live there are powerful, the cities are fortified and large, and the descendants of Anak (men of great stature, giants) are there. In describing the people of the land of Canaan, they mention that the Amalekites are in the south. The Amalekites were descendants of Esau who formed wild roving bands which infested the whole country. They mention the Amorites and Hittites who dwelt in the mountains. These two peoples were two of the powers in the land of Canaan. They mention the Canaanites who dwelt by the sea and by the coast of Jordan.

Why were the words of their report so negative? Because they had allowed themselves to take on a negative perspective. They perceived that the people of Canaan were too strong for them to defeat so it would not be wise to go up against them (v.31). Their perception was based on what they saw with their eyes but yet had they not seen the luscious fruit of the land also which they had in their possession which was a confirmation to them of God's truthfulness.

You see this is where perception is a personal choice and ten of the spies chose to take on a negative perspective. It's almost as if they had completely forgotten what God had promised to them once they explored the land of Canaan and saw how strong the people were there.

This is the danger of choosing to take on a negative perception because it can even cloud one's remembrance of what God promised to do for them. A negative perspective then leads to speaking forth negative words which simply reinforce one's negative perspective.

But look now at how different the perspective was of two of the other spies. The report that Joshua and Caleb gave was based on a positive perspective that they chose to take. In verse 30, after Joshua and Caleb stilled the people, they said "We should go up and take possession of the land, for we can certainly do it." Instead of focusing on the obstacles in the land, their focus was on God's promises and that He would drive out the inhabitants of the land from before them. All they had to do was enter the land and trust in God's promises. Their positive perspective enabled them to speak overcoming words of victory and their positive words reinforced the positive belief that they had.

When we step out by faith to explore the opportunities that God has provided for us, we will inevitably encounter obstacles in our exploration. We may see that there is a lack of resources, lack of support, potential problems with certain people, etc . . . But yet it's not the obstacles themselves that cause us to take on a negative perspective but rather a loss of focus. When facing obstacles in exploring God's opportunities for our lives, many times we focus on the obstacles and this inevitably leads to a negative perspective which leads to negative words that reinforce the negative perspective. We must be determined that no matter how great the obstacles are that we face that we will stay focused on God's promises in His word and what He has personally spoken into our hearts.

The Bible compares the tongue to the rudder of a huge ship. Although the rudder is small, it controls the direction of the entire ship, and, in a similar manner, our tongues control the direction of our lives. If we take on a negative perspective and begin to speak forth negative words, we are going to move in the direction of those words. If we tell ourselves we can't because of the obstacles before us, we will become discouraged and will not have the willpower to even try to fulfill God's will. We defeat ourselves with our words before we even get started and talk ourselves out of doing something great for God. We need to take the word "can't" completely out of our vocabulary.

If anyone faced tremendous obstacles as they stepped out to fulfill God's will, it was the Apostle Paul. Wherever Paul went, he faced adversity—beatings, hunger, arrest, imprisonment, rejection, etc. Yet he was able to keep a positive perspective. How? Because he chose to focus on God's promises instead of the obstacles before him. Paul's positive perspective is what enabled him to say "I CAN do all things through Christ who strengthens me."

Joyce Meyer from her best selling book, *Battlefield of the Mind,* writes how our thoughts become our words:

> There are thousands upon thousands of thoughts presented to us every day. The mind has to be renewed to follow after the Spirit and not the flesh. Our carnal (worldly, fleshly) minds have had so much practice operating freely that we surely don't have to use any effort to think wrong thoughts. On the other hand, we have to purposely choose right thinking. After we have finally decided to be like-minded with God, then we will need to choose and to continue to choose right thoughts. When we begin to

feel that the battle of the mind is just too difficult and that we aren't going to make it, then we must be able to cast down that kind of thinking and choose to think that we are going to make it! Not only must we choose to think that we are going to make it, but we must also decide not to quit. Bombarded with doubts and fears, we must take a stand and say: "I will never give up! God is on my side, He loves me, and He is helping me!" You and I will have many choices to make throughout our lives. In Deuteronomy 30:19 the Lord told His people that He had set before them life and death and urged them to choose life. And in Proverbs 18:21 we are told, Death and life are in the power of the tongue, and they who indulge in it shall eat the fruit of it . . . Our thoughts become our words. Therefore, it is vitally important that we choose life-generating thoughts. When we do, right words will follow.[1]

On the other hand (like Joshua and Caleb), when we choose to take on a positive perspective and begin to speak forth positive words, we then begin to move in the direction of those words—moving forward into God's will for our lives. The motivation to move forward into God's promises must come from within us and what create that inner motivation are the words that we speak. If we tell ourselves that we can do something, then our subconscious minds hear that and begin to act on that bringing it to pass.

We see in the confrontation that David had with Goliath how a positive perspective enables us to speak positive words that move us forward into victory. Goliath we know was an enormous man, about 9 feet 9 inches tall (the NBA would sure love to have him today). Not only that, but his body was covered with a coat of mail, he had bronze greaves to protect his shins, an enormous spear, and a shield about the size of a grown man to protect his whole body against the arrows of an enemy. What an imposing man he was and his words of defiance made him even more imposing to the army of Israel who had convinced themselves that Goliath could not be defeated. Their negative perspective paralyzed them with fear that kept them at a standstill.

David, however, took on a different perspective—Goliath was too big to miss. The same God who delivered the lion and bear into his hand would also deliver this uncircumcised man into his hand. His positive perspective then enabled him to speak forth faith-filled words. "David said to the Philistine, "You come against me with sword and spear and javelin, but I come against you in the name of the Lord Almighty, the God of the armies of Israel, whom you have defied. This day the Lord will deliver you into my hands . . ." (I Samuel 17:45-46). It was David's words of authority that then spurred him on to sling the stone that would slay Goliath.

There is a story of a young man who was sent to a remote part of Africa to represent a shoe company. After just a short time there, the young man came back to the manager of the company. He was discouraged and very disillusioned. "Why was I sent to that place? No one there wears shoes!" Some time later, another young man was sent to the same part of Africa. Upon his arrival there, the young man quickly ran to the telegraph office and sent back a telegram to his manager: "Please send thousands of shoes. No one here has shoes!" The first sales representative was blinded by circumstances; the second saw a golden opportunity. The difference in the two was "how they looked at things" or their perspective.

Robert Kennedy once said: "Some people see things as they are and say, 'Why?' Others see things as they could be and say, 'Why not?'

We all have the power of choice but the choices we make are truly controlled by what our perceptions are.

Psychologists tell us that there are three distinct functions of the brain: the mind, the emotions, and the will. The emotions and will determine one's character, or what others see him to be; however, the emotions and will are controlled by the mind. In other words, what the mind receives, assimilates, and stores up activates emotionalism and the power of choice. So what we see, what we hear, and what we assimilate is an input that influences the thoughts of our minds; and our minds determine our actions.

This is why there can be two groups of people in the same exact situation with the same opportunities, but one group of people says it cannot be done but the other group of people says it can. What was the difference? Their perception of what the opportunity offered.

Obstacles Appearing Much Larger Than What They Really Are

Numbers 13:32-33, "And they spread among the Israelites a bad report about the land they had explored. They said, 'The land we explored devours those living in it. All the people we saw there are of great size. We saw the Nephilim there (the descendants of Anak come from the Nephilim). We seemed like grasshoppers in our own eyes, and we looked the same to them.'"

After Joshua and Caleb gave a positive report, the 10 spies spoke up again with an even more exaggerated account of the greatness of their enemies. They said that the land of Canaan was a land that ate up the inhabitants thereof; it was a land that was exposed to attacks from every position and so the occupants would have to always be armed and on guard. But this was an exaggeration because Canaan had many hills and trees and caves that would have provided a measure of some safety from the attacks of enemy forces. They also said that they saw men of great size there who made them appear as grasshoppers. Although the sons of Anak were undoubtedly taller, the comparison they made in their stature was highly exaggerated. It was almost as if they were exaggerating what they saw in an attempt to discount the positive report of Joshua and Caleb and to make more convincing their own report.

But we also do the same things with ourselves. To convince ourselves that we can't do something, we will speak words that will make our obstacles appear to be much larger than what they really are. We can make a mountain out of a molehill simply by the words that we speak. Our obstacles then appear to be so large to us that they look impossible to overcome.

I remember an incident in my life when I did this. I was asked to sing in a Sunday night service; I agreed, although hesitantly. I had not sung for a long time but God had been laying a song on my heart for a while, so I took this invitation as a confirmation that I was supposed to sing.

I practiced every day for the next week on a particular song but when I did, I perceived the worst. I pictured myself forgetting the words of the song, getting out of key, and hyperventilating once I got up there to sing. All these negative thoughts ran through my mind in the days before I was to sing. I even had myself convinced that when the people heard me sing that one by one they would leave the service. You talk about blowing things out of proportion, but this is what false perceptions do.

What made it worse was when I began to vocalize my perceptions of what could happen, this just created more fear inside me.

Well the night came and as I stood before the people in the church to sing, I closed my eyes so I would not see the look of dismay on their faces and not see the people leave one by one. To my surprise, I did finish my song without hyperventilating and when I opened my eyes, nobody had left. They even gave me a handclap as I left the platform.

What a relief it was when I sat down and all the butterflies in my stomach began to fly away. I thought, "Here I spent all week thinking the worst about what would happen and exactly the opposite happened."

But what is ironic is that no matter how great and big that we say that God is, we can never exaggerate in this. God is so much greater and bigger than we could ever imagine or put into words yet we imply by our words sometimes how much greater our obstacles are than almighty God. Instead of speaking about how great our obstacles are why not speak about how much greater that God is. This will keep us from exaggerating about our obstacles and will keep things in proper perspective.

This is what Paul did in Asia as he wrote, "We do not want you to be uninformed, brothers and sisters, about the troubles we experienced in the province of Asia. We were under great pressure, far beyond our ability to endure, so that we despaired of life itself. Indeed, we felt we had received the sentence of death. But this happened that we might not rely on ourselves but on God, who raises the dead. He has delivered us from such a deadly peril, and he will deliver us again. On him we have set our hope that he will continue to deliver us" (II Corinthians 1:8-10).

During the first few years at one of my pastorates, I found myself being defeated often by my own words. I kept telling God how great the obstacles were that I was facing—that the church was not growing, that we did not have enough workers, we did not have enough financial resources to do outreach to the community, etc. The words that I spoke made the obstacles appear to be much larger than what they really were. Finally one day, God spoke to me clearly and told me "Instead of telling me how great your obstacles are and what is not happening, why don't you start telling me how great I am and what you believe I can do." You talk about a wake up call!

The Powerful Influence of Our Words on Others

Numbers 14:1-4, "That night, all the members of the community raised their voices and wept aloud. All the Israelites grumbled against Moses and Aaron, and the whole assembly said to them, 'If only we had died in Egypt! Or in this wilderness! Why is the Lord bringing us to this land only to let us fall by the sword? Our wives and children will be taken as plunder. Wouldn't it be better for us to go back to Egypt?' And they said to each other, 'We should choose a leader and go back to Egypt.'"

After hearing the ten spies dismal negative report twice but with even more exaggeration the second time, it caused the people of Israel to cry out with great lament and to weep all night long. The negative reports made them very sad because they had high hopes of entering into Canaan and forming their own identity as a people and now they would not have that opportunity. The negative reports also led them to murmur and complain to Moses and Aaron that they would rather have died in Egypt than to have to die out in the wilderness, and, therefore, they would choose a leader and return to Egypt.

This account really does show the powerful influence of words not only on us but on others.

Here just a day or two earlier, the people of Israel were excited about the opportunity of entering into Canaan, a land of plenty, where they would begin to raise their families and farm the land and have a land that they could call their own. Now some three million people were influenced by the negative words of just ten people to forsake this great opportunity and return to a place where they were once slaves. This shows just how powerful negative words can be in influencing people to do the wrong thing—the negative words of ten spies had a greater influence on the people than the positive words of two spies.

It has been said that for one negative word of confession, it takes approximately twenty words of faith to counteract the negative effect and change the action. Negativity breeds negativity. You stay around a negative person long enough and you will find yourself becoming negative. The spirit of negativity that is on them will jump on you.

In a church that I once attended in our Sunday evening services, we had a lady who would always testify about how sick she was all the time and how the devil was constantly defeating her. Her negative testimonies always came right before the song service and really dampened my spirit to the point that I had a hard time rejoicing as I sang. After several Sunday nights of hearing negativity spew from her mouth, I finally stood to my feet and proclaimed that we were there that night to give God all the glory and not the devil. After that the pastor told the church that unless they could testify of something good that God was doing in their lives, they should not testify at all. We had some very good testimonies after that and the worship times got a lot better too.

Positive words, however, can also have an influence on people—a positive influence. When we tell people that we have confidence in them and we believe they have what it takes to accomplish something great for God, those very words can be the very motivation that they will need to accomplish it. You see we have a tendency to try and live up to the expectations that people have in us because we want to make them proud and not let them down.

So when we begin to explore the opportunities that God has promised to us, let's make the choice to take on a positive perspective and stay focused on God's promises. That positive perspective will then enable us to speak positive words of what we believe God is going to do which will propel us forward into possession of God's promises. Make the right choice. Allow your words to work for you, not against you. Our words do have a powerful influence on people; let's choose to have a positive influence and not a negative influence.

Challenge Questions:

1) Do you have a tendency, as you seek to fulfill God's purpose for your life, to allow obstacles to create a negative perspective in your mind? If so, what can you do to prevent this?
2) How does your perspective of things affect the very words you speak?
3) What can you do to prevent your obstacles to fulfilling God's purpose for your life from appearing larger than what they really are?
4) Why is it vital that you stay away from negative people if you are to fulfill God's purpose for your life?

Chapter 5

STEAMY HOT TO A COOL BREEZE
I Samuel 25:1-35

O UR WORDS ARE MORE POWERFUL than we could ever imagine, whether for good or for bad. What makes them so powerful is that they influence one's attitudes and even their actions towards others. Words lead people to do things that they may regret for the rest of their lives.

According to the 2009 United States Crime Rates Report, there were 806,843 reported aggravated assaults and 15,241 reported murders. Typically, these crimes began with a minor disagreement between two people which led to anger, which, when it is unrestrained and influenced by the sinful nature of man, becomes rage. Do you or someone you know always seem to end up in volatile situations due to minor disagreements?

Anger becomes destructive when it persists in the form of aggression, unforgiveness, or revenge. But is all anger bad?

Anger we know is a common human emotion and it generates physical and emotional energy called adrenalin that helps us deal with hurts, threats, or frustration.

Also, anger can be constructive when it motivates us to correct injustices. The Bible mentions that God got angry. But His anger was not out of control. God has a righteous indignation against all sin and injustice. This is the type of anger that Jesus displayed when He drove the moneychangers from the temple.

There will be times that as Christians we will experience righteous indignation when we read about the number of abortions that are taking place in America or the sexual abuse of little children. Our anger is controlled in the sense that we don't seek to get revenge on those who commit such acts. But our anger should move us to make our voice known and to pray.

In this chapter, we will look at the steamy hot nature of uncontrolled anger and the steps we can take to cool someone's boiling hot anger toward us.

The Effects of Steamy Hot Anger

I Samuel 25:1-13, "Now Samuel died, and all Israel assembled and mourned for him; and they buried him at his home in Ramah. Then David moved down into the Desert of Paran. A certain man in Maon, who had property there at Carmel, was very wealthy. He had a thousand goats and three thousand sheep, which he was shearing in Carmel. His name was Nabal and his wife's name was Abigail. She was an intelligent and beautiful woman, but her husband was surly and mean in his dealings—he was a Calebite. While David was in the wilderness, he heard that Nabal was shearing sheep. So he sent ten young men and said to them, "Go up to Nabal at Carmel and greet him in my name. Say to him: 'Long life to you! Good health to you and your household! And good health to all that is yours! '"Now I hear that it is sheep-shearing time. When your shepherds were with us, we did not mistreat them, and the whole time they were at

Carmel nothing of theirs was missing. Ask your own servants and they will tell you. Therefore be favorable toward my men, since we come at a festive time. Please give your servants and your son David whatever you can find for them.'" When David's men arrived, they gave Nabal this message in David's name. Then they waited. Nabal answered David's servants, "Who is this David? Who is this son of Jesse? Many servants are breaking away from their masters these days. Why should I take my bread and water, and the meat I have slaughtered for my shearers, and give it to men coming from who knows where?" David's men turned around and went back. When they arrived, they reported every word. David said to his men, "Each of you strap on your sword!" So they did, and David strapped his on as well. About four hundred men went up with David, while two hundred stayed with the supplies."

When David heard that Nabal was shearing his sheep, he sent his men down to collect remuneration for the services he provided Nabal in protecting his shepherds from the attacks of wild tribes who sought at that time to steal the livestock. According to the custom of those days, it was a common courtesy for the owner of the sheep to set aside a part of the profit he made at the time the sheep were sheered and give to the person who provided his shepherds protection when they were out in the fields. The owner was not required to do so but it was a nice gesture of gratitude. When David's men come to collect the remuneration, Nabal refuses to pay anything. Matter of fact, he responds with, *Who is David? Why should I take the food that I have killed for my shearers and give it to someone that I don't know?* It's not like giving a little food to David for his services of protection would have hurt him financially when you consider that he owned 3,000 sheep and 1,000 goats. Nabal was, by the standards at that time, a very rich man. This was nothing but an act of ingratitude on Nabal's part.

As might be expected, when David's men returned and told him of Nabal's refusal, David grew angry. David's anger came about because he felt that he had been treated unfairly by Nabal. Here David had gone out of his way to protect Nabal's livestock and all he got in return were words of ridicule from a very ungrateful man.

Not only did David get angry, but he allowed his anger to become steamy hot. He commanded four hundred of his soldiers to gird themselves with swords and go out with him to get justice on Nabal. Taking so many men to kill one greedy man showed that David's anger had gotten so out of control that he wanted to get the ultimate revenge.

As in this account with David, anger begins in one's heart from the feeling that they have not been treated fairly in some way.

From time to time, we all experience such anger, since anger is a common human emotion. Ephesians 4:26, "In your anger do not sin . . ." Feeling such anger in its beginning stages is not necessarily sinful but it is rather how we respond to the anger that becomes critical. Anger involves both an inner reaction and an outward response. How one responds depends on who is in control—the individual or the anger itself.

Some people choose to respond to their feelings of anger by repressing it. This is anger unexpressed. They repress their anger out of shame or punishment and probably do so because it's a way that they can hold a grudge. They are then able to replay the hurt done to them. Repression of anger, however, can be dangerous because it is just like a time bomb that is getting ready to explode since anger increases rather than decreases when it is repressed. Repressed anger usually leads to bitterness and other mental, emotional, and physical fatigues and stresses.

Others, like David, choose to respond to their feelings of anger by expressing it. They feel that they have the right to get even since they were the one who was wronged. They feel the immediate need to defend themselves.

Ventilating one's anger, however, impairs one's judgment and leads to saying and doing things that they may later regret. Researchers have discovered that ventilating anger does not reduce anger but actually increases feelings of anger.

You see, expressing out-of-control anger leads to sin. Proverbs 14:17 says "A quick-tempered person does foolish things." When one reacts with anger toward the person who treated them unfairly, it just creates more friction and can even lead to acts of violence. Now you have steamy hot anger coming from both sides.

Anger expressed out of control is one of the major causes of marital discord today. It causes walls of resentment to be built up to such a degree that attempts at future communication puts both partners on the defensive which then leads to power struggles to see who can get the upper hand. There is a wise saying that goes, "Swallowing angry words before you say them is better than having to eat them afterwards." I have had many times in my own marriage that I wish I had swallowed my angry words before I said them.

John McClure wrote that it's our perception of experiences and interpretation of words and actions that determines our reaction to anger:

> As in other emotions, our thinking strongly influences our
> development of anger. How we perceive our experiences
> and how we interpret the words and actions of others will
> help determine whether or not we will react in anger.
> What arouses anger in one person may not affect another.
> Our thinking, our expectations, and our mind-set strongly
> affect our emotions, including anger.[1]

Many years ago, I wanted to show my wife how much I loved her so I decided to give her a big hug when she walked through the door.

Well, when she walked through the door and as I had my arms out ready to embrace her, she walked right by me without saying a word. In just an instant, my feelings of great exhilaration turned instantly to feelings of confusion and anger. How could she just walk right by me and not even say a word when I was waiting for her right at the door when she entered? What did I say to her in the morning before she went to work that made her so upset at me?

As I began to think what I might have said or did that morning, nothing really stood out to me that would have brought this kind of reaction from her. So I began to feel I was being unfairly treated. I had not done anything wrong. As I continued to stew at the kitchen table for over an hour, I even began to imagine the worst—that my wife was going to leave me.

I felt God leading me to go upstairs and ask her what was wrong, but my foolish pride would not allow me to. I began to reason that I had every right to be angry at her.

Finally, after battling with my own personal feelings and conviction for harboring such feelings, I finally relented my manly pride and went upstairs and sat down by my wife and asked her what was wrong. As soon as I did, she began to cry and opened up to me about the bad day that she had at work. Her boss at that time seemed to have it in for her and did things to irritate her. I then tried to comfort her and reassure her that everything would be okay.

But how foolish I felt afterwards for harboring anger at my wife because I thought she was upset at me when in reality it had nothing to do with me. How damaging that would have been to her if I had gone up stairs and spewed my angry words at her for what I thought was inconsideration on her part. My words of anger could have crushed her even more. How thankful I have been that I was able to swallow my angry words before I said them. I learned a lesson in this incident that just because someone appears to be upset does not necessarily mean that they are upset at me. They may just be having a bad day. We should always try to give people the benefit of the doubt before jumping to conclusions.

Cooling Down Steamy Hot Anger

I Samuel 25:14-31: "One of the servants told Abigail, Nabal's wife, "David sent messengers from the wilderness to give our master his greetings, but he hurled insults at them. Yet these men were very good to us. They did not mistreat us, and the whole time we were out in the fields near them nothing was missing. Night and day they were a wall around us the whole time we were herding our sheep near them. Now think it over and see what you can do, because disaster is hanging over our master and his whole household. He is such a wicked man that no one can talk to him." Abigail acted quickly. She took two hundred loaves of bread, two skins of wine, five dressed sheep, five seahs of roasted grain, a hundred cakes of raisins and two hundred cakes of pressed figs, and loaded them on donkeys. Then she told her servants, "Go on ahead; I'll follow you." But she did not tell her husband Nabal. As she came riding her donkey into a mountain ravine, there were David and his men descending toward her, and she met them. David had just said, "It's been useless—all my watching over this fellow's property in the wilderness so that nothing of his was missing. He has paid me back evil for good. May God deal with David, be it ever so severely, if by morning I leave alive one male of all who belong to him!" When Abigail saw David, she quickly got off her donkey and bowed down before David with her face to the ground. She fell at his feet and said: "Pardon your servant, my lord, and let me speak to you; hear what your servant has to say. Please pay no attention, my lord, to that wicked man Nabal. He is just like his name—his name means Fool, and folly goes with him. And as for me, your servant, I did not see the men my lord sent. And now, my lord, as surely as the Lord your God lives and as you live, since the Lord has kept you from bloodshed and from avenging yourself with your own hands, may your enemies and all who are intent on harming my lord be like Nabal. And let this gift, which your servant has brought to my lord, be given to the men who follow you. "Please forgive your servant's presumption. The Lord your God will certainly make a lasting dynasty for my lord, because you fight the Lord's battles, and no wrongdoing will be found in you as long as you live. Even though someone is pursuing you to take your life, the life of my lord will be bound securely in the bundle of the living by the Lord your God, but the lives of your enemies he will hurl away as from the pocket of a sling. When the Lord has fulfilled for my lord every good thing he promised concerning him and has appointed him ruler over Israel, my lord will not have on his conscience the staggering burden of needless bloodshed or of having avenged himself. And when the Lord your God has brought my lord success, remember your servant."

As David came with his armed men to the house of Nabal, his anger was steamy hot and boiling over. David's intention was to not only kill Nabal but also all those that pertained to his household before the morning light (v.22). When we consider the steamy hot nature of David's anger, how exactly did such steamy hot anger that was boiling over become cooled down?

A message is delivered to Abigail, the wife of Nabal, that David and his men were coming to do battle with her husband and also all those in his household. The message came to Abigail and not Nabal because he was not approachable (v.17). She is informed as to the reason why David is coming to do battle: David and his men had done well in protecting the sheep of her husband, yet when David sent his men to receive remuneration for their services, Nabal had scorned them.

But notice how Abigail, a woman of great wisdom, responded to the message and sought to appease the anger of David.

First of all, in haste, she prepares a gift of foods and livestock to be sent before her to David. In this case, she needed to act in favor of her husband and not say a word to him for she knew that he would never have approved of her actions. By sending the gift out first, she sought to appease some of David's anger so when she approached him, he would be more receptive to what she would say.

The first step to appease someone's anger towards us is through the gift of prayer. Proverbs 21:14 says "A gift given in secret soothes anger . . ."

We offer up to God our prayers in secret on behalf of ourselves and for the person who is angry at us with the intent of reconciliation.

Prayer for ourselves at this point is vital because it allows us to get our own emotions under control first before we try to reconcile with the person who is angry at us. So we offer prayer up for ourselves first. This is one way that we become slow to anger. ". . . but the one who is patient calms a quarrel" (Proverbs 15:18).

But then we also offer up our prayers on behalf of those who are angry at us by asking God to prepare their hearts to be receptive when we approach them to reconcile.

The Bible gives high praise to those who are slow to anger. "Better a patient person than a warrior, one with self-control than one who takes a city" (Proverbs 16:32).

So it is better to use our words constructively by praying in secret for God's divine intervention than to use them destructively through using our own human intervention to defend our rights.

Best selling author, Charles Swindoll, writes that we need to be wise when conflicts arise:

> First of all, whatever you do when conflicts arise, be wise. If you're not careful, you will handle conflicts in the energy of the flesh. And then . . . you'll be sorry. What do I mean by being wise? Well, look at the whole picture. Fight against jumping to quick solutions and seeing only your side. Look both ways. Weigh the differences. There are always two sides on the streets of conflict. Look both ways. Weigh the differences. The other part of being wise is to pray. Get God's perspective. He gives us the wisdom we need when we ask Him for it.[2]

Second of all, as Abigail approaches David, she falls on her face before him at his feet as a token of humility and reverence, and asks that the iniquity of her husband be laid on her. She relates to him that when he sent his men to her husband, she was not there to offer another response. Then she asks him to forgive her trespasses. In essence, she was asking David for forgiveness for the actions of her husband.

So the second step in appeasing the anger that someone has for us is through giving a soft answer. Proverbs 15:1 says, "A gentle answer turns away wrath . . ." As we approach the person who is angry at us, we should do so with a humble spirit and then simply apologize for any hurt that we may have caused them. It takes a bigger man or woman to apologize and say that they are sorry than someone who won't. We should still go and apologize even if we feel that the person has no legitimate reason for being angry at us. It's still the right thing to do and the quickest way to clear up any misunderstandings and to defuse the other person's anger.

John Bevere writes concerning how an offended person's understanding is darkened:

> No matter what caused it, this offended person's understanding is darkened, and he has based his judgments on assumptions, hearsay and appearances, deceiving himself even though he believes he has discerned our true motives. How can we have an accurate judgment without accurate information? We must be sensitive to the fact that he believes with his whole heart that he has been wronged. For whatever reason he feels this way, we must be willing to humble ourselves and apologize.[3]

This soft answer involves not only what we say, but how we say it. What we say is important but also how we say it, the tone of voice that we use, makes a difference as to the acceptance of what we say. You see we could tell someone that we are sorry but if it is done with a harsh tone, it won't be accepted. The other person must sense that our apology is genuine and sincere before they will accept it. You can sense that Abigail's apology to David was done in a soft and calm manner.

Third, she advises David that since one day he would be king, it would not be wise to ruin his record with a murder. She relates that she did not want to see this revengeful act that David was proposing to bring such guilt to his own heart that it would be a stumbling block to him when he would administer justice as the king of Israel some day.

So the third step in appeasing the anger that someone has for us is to tell them why the anger should be set aside. Let them know we appreciate them as a person and what their friendship means to us.

Let them know that we value their friendship so highly that we don't want anything to come between us that could ruin that friendship.

Steamy Hot Anger to a Cool Breeze

I Samuel 25:32-35, "David said to Abigail, 'Praise be to the Lord, the God of Israel, who has sent you today to meet me. May you be blessed for your good judgment and for keeping me from bloodshed this day and from avenging myself with my own hands. Otherwise, as surely as the Lord, the God of Israel, lives, who has kept me from harming you, if you had not come quickly to meet me, not one male belonging to Nabal would have been left alive by daybreak.' Then David accepted from her hand what she had brought him and said, "Go home in peace. I have heard your words and granted your request.""

We see here that because of Abigail's actions, the steamy hot anger of David turned into a cool breeze. Just like the steamy hot effects of a scorching sun are suddenly not felt when a cool breeze blows by, so it was with David's anger. Notice how much more cool, collected, and calm David was after his anger was appeased. He acknowledges that it was God who had sent Abigail to him that day. He commends Abigail for her advice which prevented him from surely murdering Nabal and his household, a murder that he would have regretted. Finally, he accepts Abigail's present and dismisses her with the assurance that all was forgiven.

This story is a perfect example of the influence of words on ourselves and others. Our words do have the power to appease the steamy hot anger that someone may have toward us. Our words can either add more heat to their steamy hot anger or they can bring their steamy hot anger to a cool breeze where they are no longer angry but rather calm, cool, and collected, and ready to make peace.

As we approach those who are angry at us with a soft answer by apologizing and asking them to forgive us, it takes away their reason for being angry at us and thus appeases their wrath. When we approach them with a soft tone of voice, they are more apt to listen to what we have to say, which can appease their wrath. When we tell them how much we appreciate them and their friendship, it reaffirms to them how sincere we are in reconciling with them and this can appease their anger. Where once there was strife, there are now peaceful relations. Where once there was steamy hot, there is now a cool breeze. Yes, our words have influence on others to appease their anger.

Challenge Questions:

1) Is all anger bad? Explain.
2) How does anger involve both an inner reaction and an outward response?
3) What are two harmful ways that you could respond to some one who has made you angry and why are such responses so harmful?
4) What are three ways that you could appease the anger that someone has towards you?

Chapter 6

YOU POSSESS WHAT'S CONFESSED
Romans 4:16-25

I T IS TRUE THAT WE possess what we confess. When we confess something long enough, our subconscious minds begin to act on what we are confessing until those words are brought to pass. For instance, if a person confesses long enough that they are sick when really they aren't, eventually their subconscious mind will act on those words and bring sickness. On the other hand, if a person confesses long enough that they are thankful for what they have, their subconscious mind will act on those words and bring feelings of gratefulness.

Words are similar to seeds. By speaking them out loud to where we can hear those words, they become implanted in our subconscious minds where they take root and produce the fruit of what is spoken. So if we are producing bad fruit in our lives, maybe we need to check to see what kind of seeds we are planting by our words. The fact is, we move in the direction of our words. We reap what we sow with our words.

In relation to us reaping God's promises in our lives, how vital it is that we speak forth those promises as they become the seeds that are then planted in our minds and hearts which then lead to reaping.

Best-selling author Charles Capps refers to Christianity as The Great Confession:

> Christianity is called the great confession, but most Christians who are defeated in life are defeated because they believe and confess the wrong things. They have spoken the words of the enemy. And those words hold them in bondage. Proverbs 6:2 says, "You have been trapped by what you said, ensnared by the words of your mouth." Faith filled words will put you over. Fear filled words will defeat you.[1]

In this chapter, we will see how our confession of God's promises without wavering is what will enable us to possess those promises.

Attaining Salvation through Faith

Romans 4:16: "Therefore, the promise comes by faith, so that it may be by grace and may be guaranteed to all Abraham's offspring—not only to those who are of the law but also to those who have the faith of Abraham. He is the father of us all."

Based on the reasoning of what he had already written, Paul writes we have come to this conclusion that salvation is by faith that it might be by grace. Grace is the undeserved mercy of God. If people could be saved by the works of the law then it would be through their own efforts and merits that they were saved and would no longer be by grace. But because sinners are saved by faith and not works, their salvation is only made possible because of God's unmerited favor.

Ephesians 2:8-9, "For it is by grace you have been saved, through faith (and this is not from yourselves, it is the gift of God) not by works, so that no one can boast."

There are many theories and opinions as to what is required to receive salvation, but the Bible takes away the confusion and states exactly what is required.

This passage in Romans 4:16 tells us that salvation is attained through faith, but what all does that entail?

Romans 10:8-10 says, "But what does it say? 'The word is near you; it is in your mouth and in your heart,' that is, the message concerning faith that we proclaim: If you declare with your mouth, 'Jesus is Lord,' and believe in your heart that God raised him from the dead, you will be saved. For it is with your heart that you believe and are justified, and it is with your mouth that you profess your faith and are saved."

Faith is produced in our hearts and comes from hearing the Word of God. However, once faith has come into the heart, it must then be acted on if it is to be effective. One way that one acts on their faith is by confessing that faith with their mouth. So as Paul defines the basic requirements for salvation, he laid equal stress on faith in the heart and confession with the mouth. In verse 10, Paul writes that with the heart, man believes he can be right with God because Jesus has already died for his sins and was raised from the dead. He then confesses this belief in his heart through his mouth. He confesses that he is a sinner in need of salvation but because Jesus died for his sins and rose again, he can be saved. His confession of this belief proves that the faith in his heart is genuine and is what enables him to be saved by God's grace.

Derek Prince, one of America's best-known Christian teachers, describes this connection between our mouths and our hearts:

> The whole Bible emphasizes that there is a direct connection between our mouths and our hearts. What

happens in the one can never be separated from what happens in the other. In Matthew 12:34, Jesus told us, "For the mouth speaks out of that which fills the heart." Today's English Version renders this, "For the mouth speaks what the heart is full of." In other words, the mouth is the overflow valve of the heart. Whatever comes out through that overflow valve indicates the contents of the heart.[2]

Speaking of Things as Already Done

Romans 4:17: As it is written: "I have made you a father of many nations. He is our father in the sight of God, in whom he believed—the God who gives life to the dead and calls into being things that were not."

When God spoke to Abraham that he would be the father to many descendants even though his wife Sarah was barren, He spoke of it as already done. In God's divine purpose, he constituted Abraham the father of many nations and so certain was the fulfillment of the divine purpose, that God spoke of it as already accomplished.

Thus, God speaks of things as already done through faith. When God has a divine purpose for our lives, He speaks to our hearts concerning that purpose as it is already done. He calls those things which be not as though they were. When God foretells us things and gives us promises, it is so certain to Him that it will occur that He speaks of them as already in existence.

Hebrews 11:3 says, "By faith we understand that the universe was formed at God's command, so that what is seen was not made out of what is visible."

In reading the creation account in Genesis 1, the method God used in creation was the power of His word. Over and over it is stated, "And God said" . . . let there be light and there was light; let there be a firmament and there was a firmament; let the waters be gathered together in one place and it was so." He spoke these things into existence, into an earth that was empty and formless. Each time that God spoke He released His faith—the creative power to bring His words to pass.

By speaking of things as though they already exist, God is exemplifying to believers how the principle of faith operates; by speaking forth the existence of things before they are actually seen and how the speaking forth of faith filled words allows things which be not to come into existence.

Paul says that it is God who gives life to the dead but why would Paul use that phrase here? It probably had reference to the strong natural improbability of the fulfillment of the prophecy when it was given to Abraham, arising from the age of Abraham and Sarah and that Sarah was now past the age of being able to have children. If God, however, could raise up the dead from the grave, would He not also have the power to open up Sarah's womb so that she could bear children despite her age? The fact is with God, all things are possible.

Maintaining the Right Confession

Romans 4:18-21: "Against all hope, Abraham in hope believed and so became the father of many nations, just as it had been said to him, 'So shall your offspring be.' Without weakening in his faith, he faced the fact that his body was as good as dead—since he was about a hundred years old—and that Sarah's womb was also dead. Yet he did not waver through unbelief regarding the promise of God, but was strengthened in his faith and gave glory to God, being fully persuaded that God had power to do what he had promised."

Abraham, who against all apparent or usual grounds of hope, believed in hope (v.18). How could Abraham maintain such hope despite having nothing in the natural to base his hope in? Because he chose to not base his hope in what man said was not possible but rather in what God said was possible. God had told him that his descendants would be as the stars of heaven in multitude in Genesis 15:5.

You see whatever we base our hope in will determine the validity of that hope. Hebrews 11:1 says, "Now faith is confidence in what we hope for and assurance about what we do not see." Hope by itself has no substance; by itself it is merely a dream that may or may not come to pass. But what gives hope validity and substance is our faith—a faith that is based on God's Word, the words of Him who cannot lie.

Being strong in his faith, Abraham did not allow the fact that he and Sarah were now at ages that would make having children highly improbable to influence him or to produce any doubt about its fulfillment (v.19).

So what is faith? Faith is taking God at His word, in that what He has promised He is able to fulfill. Faith has been defined as a firm persuasion and expectation that God will perform all that He has provided to us in Christ; and this persuasion is so strong that it gives the soul a kind of possession and present fruition of those things (Matthew Henry). Faith is not based in what one can see but instead in the unseen realities of God. This is the type of faith that Abraham had.

Some people say 'Show me first and then I will believe,' but this is not faith; for faith says "I will believe before I see." Hebrews 11:1 says faith is ". . . assurance about what we do not see." In other words, faith is our title deed. Anytime we can see something or perceive something with our five senses, it is not faith. It's our faith that gives reality to the existence of things hoped for. If I have evidence of something, that means I don't have the thing yet but I have substantial substance which shows the thing exists. Our faith in the unseen is what will cause the unseen to become seen.

Because of Abraham's strong faith, he did not waver at God's promises through unbelief.

Derek Prince writes concerning Abraham's unwavering faith:

> Abraham's senses told him that he was physically incapable of fathering a child and that Sarah was likewise incapable of bearing one. Yet God had promised them a son of their own. Abraham did not pretend that what his senses revealed to him about his own body and about Sarah's body was not real. He simply refused to accept it as final. When God's word promised him one thing and his senses told him another, he clung tenaciously to God's promise, without letting his senses cause him to doubt that promise. Finally, after their faith had been tested, Sarah's body was brought into line with what God had promised. They actually became physically capable of having a child.[3]

Abraham did not waver in his faith but remained strong in it and steadfastly maintained the right confession as he gave glory to God for the promise of a son. The faith in his heart of God's promise enabled him to confess it with his mouth.

He gave glory to God as he was fully persuaded that what God had promised, He could surely perform. Through his confession, he claimed the promise before he actually saw it.

In the same way we are to confess what we believe without wavering.

Hebrews 10:23 says, "Let us hold unswervingly to the hope we profess, for he who promised is faithful."

We are to confess our faith without wavering. Once we have brought the words of our mouths into agreement with God's written word, we must be careful not to change or go back to a position of unbelief. Many pressures may come against us that will try our faith and seek to weaken our confession. It may seem that things are going contrary to what we expected. At such times, our feelings may prompt us to say something that does not agree with God's word. But we persistently resist our feelings and make the words of our mouths agree with God's word. Feelings can change and waver but by our faith and our confession, we can continue to hold onto something that does not waver—God's faithfulness to fulfill His promises to us.

When my daughter Brianna was only four years old, she was at her cousin's birthday party in West Virginia (she and her mom were visiting relatives there) and as she was chasing one of her other cousins outside, she ran right into a baseball bat that was being swung.

When the accident happened, Brianna stopped breathing but her uncle prayed for her, and God restored life to her little body. She was then rushed by ambulance to the nearest hospital.

At the time of the accident, I was still in Illinois and visiting at the home of two of my members when a call came there for me. I picked up the phone with hesitancy as it was unusual that a call would have come to me there. As I said hello, I heard an unfamiliar voice and the lady said she was a nurse at a hospital in Maryland and had some bad news to share with me. Immediately, I knew that something bad had happened to either my wife Tammy or my daughter or maybe to both of them. As she began to tell me what the bad news was, I was frozen with shock. She told me that my daughter had been hit in the head with a baseball bat and that her chances of survival were not good. I don't remember if I even finished the conversation with her and said goodbye because within a matter of 15 minutes, I had driven home, thrown some clothes into a suitcase, jumped into my car, and was off for Maryland, a drive of about 17 hours.

By the time I had driven a few hours, it was getting dark and it was all I could do to stay awake. As I drove into the night, paralyzing thoughts of fear kept flooding my mind that my little girl was already dead and I would never get to see her alive again. Such thoughts caused my heart to beat more heavily and I knew that I was panicking.

Right at that moment that I didn't think I could take any more, that still small voice of God spoke to me and told me to start confessing healing over my daughter. God assured me that He would heal her if I would confess that healing. I remembered that just a little while ago that my wife Tammy had finally called me and in between her sobs told me the same report that the nurse had told me. God then asked me "Whose report will you believe – my report or what the doctors are saying?" I had a decision to make at that moment and I chose to believe the report of the Lord.

As I continued to drive at a high rate of speed (yes, I admit I was speeding), I rebuked the spirit of fear that had been trying to paralyze my faith and I started confessing my daughter's healing. "Jesus, by your stripes we are healed. Many are the afflictions of the righteous but the Lord is able to deliver them out of them all. With God all things are possible."

As I continued to confess God's promises, the fear that I had just recently been so overwhelmed with left and I felt God's peace surrounding me. You see fear cannot dwell in an atmosphere of faith. As I continued to claim God's promises of healing, I felt assured that Brianna was going to be okay.

A little later I received a call on my cell phone and, as I answered that call, I expected the best, not the worst. It really did not surprise me when my wife told me that Brianna was going to pull through.

For the rest of that trip, I just thanked God for His healing power and what He was going to continue to do for Brianna.

For the next few weeks that Brianna was in the hospital and the doctors would give us negative reports for her full recovery, we would confess God's healing power and one miracle after another would happen. To the doctor's amazement, in just a few weeks, Brianna walked out of the hospital on her own. The doctors told us that when we got her home, that she would need months of physical therapy to get her balance back, but after just one session, the physical therapist told us that there was no need to bring her back because she had perfect balance. In just three months, after the accident, Brianna was enrolled in tap dancing and was one of the top dancers in her class.

When God fulfills His promises in our lives, He does it in a way that no man could ever take the credit for what was accomplished. To God be all the glory!

When Abraham confessed his faith, he confessed what he believed in the present. He gave glory to God as if the promise was already a present reality. Through his confession, he claimed the promise before he actually saw it.

Hebrews 11:1 states that "faith is . . ." This means that God expects us to operate our faith in the present if we are to receive those things hoped for. It must be a present, abiding faith that is now. Many will say, "I believe God is going to do something in my life next year or sometime in the future." That's in the future. Others say, "God did this for me once in the past but I am not sure if He can do it again." That's in the past. We must make the decision to release faith that is in the now.

The way we do this is to confess and give glory to God for the promise as if it is a present reality like Abraham did.

Mark 11:24 states, "Therefore I tell you, whatever you ask for in prayer, believe that you have received it, and it will be yours."

This scripture is saying that right when we pray for God's promises to be fulfilled in our lives, we have to believe that we receive them. Notice that Jesus said you have what you believed you would receive. Therefore, we should pray and confess as if we already have the promise. Such faith-filled words will sound out as "God, I thank you for healing me." "God, I thank you for the revival that you have sent." "God, I thank you giving me that job."

Because Abraham did not waver in his faith but gave glory to God for the promise before he actually saw it, it created an atmosphere of faith to where God could do the miraculous. The physical condition both of Abraham's body and Sarah's body were brought into line with what God had promised even though Abraham was one hundred years old and Sarah was ninety years old at the time.

When we activate our faith by our words in giving glory to God for the promise before it is seen, we create an atmosphere of faith to where God can now do the miraculous. The right confession of faith allows the unseen to become a present reality, for the things that God has promised in the spiritual realm to be manifested in the physical realm. Our words do carry influence when it comes to faith.

Manifesting God's Righteousness

Romans 4:22-25: "This is why 'it was credited to him as righteousness.' The words 'it was credited to him' were written not for him alone, but also for us, to whom God will credit righteousness—for us who believe in him who raised Jesus our Lord from the dead. He was delivered over to death for our sins and was raised to life for our justification."

The writer says here that Abraham's faith (his strong confidence and unwavering assurance in God and His promises) is counted as righteousness (v.22) as it was full proof that he was righteous and in a right relationship with God.

This record of Abraham's strong faith that became proof of his righteousness was not made on Abraham's account only but was made to show the way in which men may be regarded as righteous by God. Like Abraham, when we are strong in the faith and continue to hold to God's promise with unwavering faith, this is proof that we have received God's righteousness because only those who are truly connected to God in a right relationship could have such unwavering faith.

In the same manner, when we were justified and forgiven of our sins, we were justified by our faith in Jesus' death and resurrection and at that time received God's righteousness.

So in conclusion, we do possess what we confess. As we confess God's promises to us and hold to that confession without wavering, our faith filled words create an atmosphere of faith in which God can do the miraculous and make our hopes a present reality. So our words can have a positive influence in creating faith that allows God to fulfill His promises to us.

Challenge Questions:

1) Why is it true that you possess what you confess?
2) When faith is produced in your heart through hearing the word of God, what must you do next for that faith to be effective?
3) Why is it vital that you continue to confess what you believe without wavering?
4) Explain how you can operate your faith in the present?

Chapter 7

A CAUGHT VISION IS A CAST VISION
Nehemiah 2:11-18

W HAT IS A VISION? A vision is a clear mental picture of what could be, fueled by the conviction that it should be. It is a destination, a goal that one hopes to achieve.

Every great work and every great person came under the influence of a vision that changed them and, therefore, changed others. Such was the vision that changed Nehemiah which led to changing others.

Nehemiah's vision came at a time in which he had a very prominent position as the king's cupbearer. This was a very trusted position as the cupbearer would taste the king's wine first to make sure it was not poisoned before it was given to the king. But being the king's cupbearer was not God's ultimate plan for Nehemiah's life, only a part of the plan.

Although things were going well in Nehemiah's life, things were not going well back in his homeland. The wall of Jerusalem had been torn down and the people there had no protection from their enemies. When Nehemiah heard about the plight of his homeland, his concern over the condition of Jerusalem and its people was so deep that it caused him to weep and mourn for several days, and drove him to a prolonged period of prayer and fasting. However, little did he know at the time that these deep feelings were the initial birth pains of a vision—a vision that would have him traveling back to Jerusalem and rebuilding the wall of Jerusalem.

A God-ordained vision will begin as a concern. Something will bother you about the way things are or the way things are headed. You will find yourself thinking about it all the time and the very thought of how things are will cause your heart to grieve and mourn. This heart-felt burden will motivate you to make sacrifices of prolonged periods of prayer and fasting as you cry out to God in desperation for needed change. It's in such seasons of prayer and fasting that God will develop a vision within you to bring about the needed change. So what started out as a concern develops into a vision.

After Nehemiah received his vision, he did not act on it right away, but he continued to pray for God to open the door by giving him favor with the king. You see without the king's permission and financial support, there was no way that he would be able to return to Jerusalem to fulfill his vision. He knew that the vision within him was a God thing and he also knew that it would have to be a God thing for the door to be opened for him to return to Jerusalem. Because Nehemiah waited on God's timing, when he asked the king for permission to return to Jerusalem, the king granted his request and also gave him financial support. Likewise, you need to also wait on God's timing before you move forward with your vision because only God knows when things are in place and ready for the vision to be fulfilled.

Investigating Before Casting

Nehemiah 2:11-16, "I went to Jerusalem, and after staying there three days I set out during the night with a few others. I had not told anyone what my God had put in my heart to do for Jerusalem.

There were no mounts with me except the one I was riding on. By night I went out through the Valley Gate toward the Jackal Well and the Dung Gate, examining the walls of Jerusalem, which had been broken down, and its gates, which had been destroyed by fire. Then I moved on toward the Fountain Gate and the King's Pool, but there was not enough room for my mount to get through; so I went up the valley by night, examining the wall. Finally, I turned back and reentered through the Valley Gate. The officials did not know where I had gone or what I was doing, because as yet I had said nothing to the Jews or the priests or nobles or officials or any others who would be doing the work."

After the long journey, three days of rest was necessary. After getting rested up, notice the carefulness of the investigation that Nehemiah took to avoid getting noticed. He goes out by night, with only a few men, and with only one beast. He was anxious to see with his own eyes the extent of the repairs needed, but wished as few people as possible to know of his proceedings. I believe Nehemiah wanted to have a thorough knowledge first of what was going to be required to make his vision possible before he cast his vision to the people who would help him fulfill it. This would require him to do a thorough investigation of the damage and what would be required to repair the wall.

Before you cast your vision to people whom you are counting on to help you fulfill it, investigate thoroughly first how the vision will be fulfilled. If you as the vision caster want people to get on board with your vision and help support it, they will want to know as many details as possible so they know what they are committing to and if they are willing to make the sacrifice. Investigation also prepares us to answer as many of their questions as possible. So it is vital that the vision caster does his homework first.

This is what good fishermen will do. They will investigate the good places to cast their lines depending on the kind of fish they are trying to catch. For some fish, it will be better to go to deep places to cast the line, but for other fish, the shallow places where there is seaweed is a good place to cast. They will also investigate the weather report to see if the conditions will be right for the fish to bite. They will investigate their tackle box to make sure they have the right bait for the kind of fish they are hoping to catch. Good fishermen do not leave to chance that they will catch fish, but they do a thorough investigation first to increase their chances of a good catch.

In his initial investigation, Nehemiah does a thorough investigation of the damage done to the walls all the way around. He needed to know the extent of the damage first before he could make plans on how to repair it.

In your initial investigation, you should also investigate thoroughly the extent of the ruins. What are the conditions that you are beginning in? For instance, if you are taking over a ministry at a church that has not grown for many years and lies in ruins, investigate thoroughly the ruins. Examine the ruins at every point and angle. What has been done and what has not been done to contribute to the ruined condition of this ministry? What is the present morale of the people who have been involved in this ministry? Are there foundational pieces in place yet that you could use to help rebuild this ministry? This process is vital because you must know what you have to work with first before you can make plans to rebuild it.

During those three days of looking at the damage, Nehemiah was also able to envision how the wall would be rebuilt. Knowing the extent of the damage, Nehemiah now knew where the builders would need to be set up and how much material would be needed. He was able to glean ideas of how to begin the rebuilding process and the step-by-step process that would be needed to complete the project.

As you investigate the ruins, you must then envision how the vision will be fulfilled. For instance, what are the steps that you will take now to rebuild this ministry? What are the greatest areas of need in this ministry that you need to focus on the most and in what areas do you ask for volunteers to help in? What resources will you need as you rebuild? In this process of envisioning, your vision becomes clearer. Before you begin to initiate a vision, you always want to make sure that you are building first on a solid foundation.

Your thorough investigation will also be a wake-up call for yourself if you are willing to pay the price that will be required to fulfill your vision. Are you willing to invest the time, resources, focus, and energy into this vision to make it happen? Yes, God will direct and empower you as you seek to fulfill your vision but only when you are willing to put forth the effort first.

Jesus said, "And whoever does not carry their cross and follow me cannot be my disciple. 'Suppose one of you wants to build a tower. Won't you first sit down and estimate the cost to see if you have enough money to complete it?'" (Luke 14:27-28). Jesus teaches here that whoever desires to follow Him and be His disciple should first decide whether they are prepared to pay the cost, much like one who is getting ready to build a tower.

Casting Your Vision

Nehemiah 2:17-18a, "Then I said to them, 'You see the trouble we are in: Jerusalem lies in ruins, and its gates have been burned with fire. Come, let us rebuild the wall of Jerusalem, and we will no longer be in disgrace.' I also told them about the gracious hand of my God on me and what the king had said to me . . ."

Even though fishermen do a thorough investigation, they will still not catch any fish until they first cast out the line. The fish are not going to swim up to the shore line and jump out of the water into their laps.

Thorough investigation is a vital process before you cast your vision but all the investigation in the world will do you no good until you first cast out your vision to those whom you are counting on for assistance. You must cast your vision if it is to be caught.

John Maxwell, an international leadership expert, describes the importance of transferring the vision to people:

> I've met a lot of people with big dreams who never achieved them because they were unable to get others to see and buy into their vision. They believed that if the dream was worthy, people would simply line up to be a part of it. Recruiting a team doesn't work that way. People who fall into this trap may be visionary, they may be hardworking, and they may have noble intentions, but they won't succeed if they don't learn how to transfer the vision to others. They are condemned to experience the curse that is reportedly used in Romania, which says, "May you have a brilliant idea, which you know is right, and be unable to convince others."[1]

But good fishermen also know that there is a proper way to cast their fishing line if they are to catch fish. I've been told by good fishermen that casting is one of the keys to catching fish. When one is fishing for walleye, for example, after casting out one's line, it is important to jiggle the line as it is being reeled in. Fly fishing requires great skill to cast the baited line into the water by manipulating the rod.

There is a certain way that you cast your vision so it will be caught by others, which you can learn from Nehemiah's vision casting.

First of all, Nehemiah's vision casting was explained clearly to the people. He was able to explain it clearly because of the thorough investigation that he had done beforehand. He told them clearly what the problem was. He did not beat around the bush about it. "You see the trouble we are in: Jerusalem lies in ruins, and its gates have been burned with fire." There was no confusion in what they were hearing. They understood clearly because it was communicated to them clearly.

Before people will support a vision, they must first be made to understand what the vision entails. Vision casters who have done their homework first and thoroughly investigated will have the advantage of speaking of something that they understand well. This is what will enable them to speak clearly about it. You cannot communicate something to others if you don't understand it clearly yourself first. But speaking clearly means that the vision caster is also plain and upfront as to the condition of things right now. This is vital because people need to see the severity of the problem first before they will do anything about it.

John Maxwell writes of this first step in gaining credibility with people:

> What people don't believe, they don't buy into. The ability to communicate your dream logically is the first step in gaining credibility with people. If you don't pass this first gate of people's intellect, you will not be able to proceed any further. How do you do that? First, by communicating a realistic understanding of the situation today. Every time you communicate vision to people, the first thing the skeptics ask is, "But what about . . . ?" If they don't ask it out loud, they say it to themselves. And they will keep asking it until you have addressed all their concerns. You need to demonstrate that you understand the situation at least as well as they do. That requires being extremely thorough when sharing your dream and

not dwelling on its positive benefits to the exclusion of the facts.[2]

For instance, a newly appointed Youth Minister might say to his team "This ministry has been in shambles for a few years now. There have been no regular meetings and there is no organization in place. Most of the youth who used to be a part of this ministry are no longer attending and the youth who are still here are discouraged."

Second, in Nehemiah's vision casting, he created a visual in the people's minds of what could be, "Come, let us rebuild the wall of Jerusalem . . ." By saying this, he was hoping that they would be able to envision in their minds Jerusalem as a walled city. Thus, he was able to make the vision real to them and a realistic endeavor.

One of the keys to transferring the vision to people is making it real to them visually. The people need to be able to see the vision if they are going to get behind it. When they can envision in their minds what the vision will result in, it becomes more realistic to them and something that can be achieved. There is a saying that a picture is worth a thousand words. Create a picture in their minds of what can be and this verbal picture will speak volumes to them.

Andy Stanley relates how the solution engages the imagination:

> Whereas a clear explanation of the problem engages the mind, the solution engages the imagination. A vision invites us to imagine the future in a way that demands change in the present. A vision necessitates a willingness on the part of the audience to overlook present reality for the time being and imagine what could be.[3]

For instance, that newly appointed Youth Minister might say to his team: "We are going to rebuild this Youth Ministry by putting procedures and job requirements into place so everyone will know what is expected of them. This will enable us to lay the foundation for a ministry that will stand. We will then begin to start our meetings up on a regular basis and contact the youth who used to attend to get them interested again. Then in one year from now, I foresee us having a thriving Youth Ministry with at least thirty youth actively involved in the ministry and regular Youth Meetings that involve dynamic worship and relevant sermons that compel the youth to pray and seek God."

Third, Nehemiah in his vision casting shared with them what the benefits would be, ". . . and we will no longer be in disgrace." Disgrace means embarrassment so he was telling them that they had been an embarrassment to the nations who surrounded them. Israel had once been known as a mighty nation and the city of Jerusalem the residence of God's glory. But now there was no more glory. With the temple destroyed and sacrifices ceased, God's glory was gone and the city of Jerusalem had no protection from its enemies with the walls being down. So Nehemiah's vision casting to them was not so much about rebuilding a wall as much as it was about rebuilding their destiny as God's chosen people. Once the walls were rebuilt, the temple could then be rebuilt and the sacrifices reinstituted and the people would have the protection they would need to carry out God's plan for them as a distinct and special people.

As you cast your vision, show the people the benefits of fulfilling the vision and how this ties in with God's purpose. Tell them that by fulfilling this vision, this is what will be accomplished for God. This will motivate them to support the vision and do what it takes to bring it to fulfillment. Seeing the benefits will help them see that this is a cause that is worth investing their time and energy into.

People need to see that the vision is something bigger than the project itself—that it has the capacity to grow into bigger circles of influence.

Giving people a reason engages their will that something should be done which then compels them to do it.

For instance, the Youth Minister might tell his team "By rebuilding this Youth Ministry and seeing it grow, we can then formulate teams of youth who will be able to go out into the community and have an impact on other youth and get involved in service projects."

Fourth, Nehemiah in his vision casting gives the people a reason why the rebuilding needed to be done now. He tells them that it was God who orchestrated the events that led to his arrival in Jerusalem. As he prayed for favor with the king, it was God who moved upon King Artaxerxes to take an interest in and support his vision. This is what happened as the king gave him financial support for the building project; he procured letters to the governors in the surrounding areas asking them to provide Nehemiah safe conduct along the way; and the king worked out a deal with Asaph, keeper of the king's forest, to procure enough lumber to build the city's gates. It was clear by these events that God had opened up the door for Nehemiah's vision to be fulfilled and they needed now to continue to move forward with it.

As you cast your vision, tell the people why the vision needs to be fulfilled now. Share with them what God has been orchestrating up to this point to fulfill the vision. This will reassure them that the timing is right to pursue the vision now because people want to be a part of something that God is up to. This will enable you and your team to move forward with the vision and not procrastinate.

Andy Stanley from his book *Visioneering* further writes:

> When you zero in on why your vision must be accomplished, you will find yourself energized by the mere thought of what you have been called to do. Why translates into urgency and incentive. And you speak

of your vision, your conviction that this is something that should be done will make you persuasive in your communication.[4]

Once again, that Youth Minister might share with his team how God laid on his heart about a year ago a burden for the youth and how during that time he had been praying and fasting for that ministry that God would bring it to life again. He had put a fleece out before God that if the Pastor asked him to take over that ministry, he would go forward with the vision that God had given him.

The Igniting Of Enthusiasm

Nehemiah 2:18b, "They replied, 'Let us start rebuilding.' So they began this good work."

Notice that after Nehemiah cast his vision to the people, that it was the people who said "Let us start rebuilding." Because Nehemiah had taken the time to investigate thoroughly the building project and formulate his plans, it enabled him to cast his vision to the people in a way that he could clearly explain it to them, help them to visually see the vision, explain the benefits of fulfilling the vision, and to explain why the timing was right to fulfill the vision. This led to the igniting of enthusiasm in the hearts of a group of people to begin a building project that they had procrastinated in doing for over one hundred years.

When you do a thorough investigation into your vision and formulate plans through that investigation on how to fulfill it, you will then be able to cast your vision in a way that will influence people to support it and help you fulfill it. The igniting of enthusiasm in their hearts will be so great that those same people who were once procrastinators will be the very ones to step forward and take the initiative in fulfilling the vision. They will take ownership of it. This is every leader's dream.

Enthusiasm comes from two Greek words, en, which means "within," and theos which means "God." So it literally means God within. When you are able to take a vision that God has planted within you and are able to share it with others in a way that it becomes planted within them as a God thing, it creates enthusiasm.

And the people got to work rebuilding the wall. They saw clearly the situation as it was, they envisioned what could be, and they felt compelled that this was something that needed to be done now. This created enthusiasm within them that gave them strength to complete the task despite the obstacles that were stacked against them. As they built, they were ridiculed, scorned, and threatened but yet they continued to build and in just fifty two days, they completed the task.

Enthusiasm will strengthen you like nothing else can as you face obstacles in the fulfillment of the vision. Satan will attack you and try to discourage you from advancing with it. But he cannot stop you because your enthusiasm is a God thing within you that will empower you to defeat every obstacle in your path.

Ralph Waldo Emerson wrote, "Nothing great was ever achieved without enthusiasm."

The fact is enthusiastic people get things done and they get them done under the harshest and most severe conditions.

Emerson also wrote, "Those folks who succeed remain enthusiastic longer than those who fall. Every great and commanding movement in the annals of the world has been the triumph of enthusiasm."

In the 1700's, a man by the name of William Carey received a vision. A cobbler by trade, he kept a map of the whole world on a wall of his workshop so he could pray for the nations of the world. He then developed a burden for a definite missionary outreach in India. When he shared this vision at a meeting of ministers, he was told by a senior man of God, "Young man, sit down. When God wants to convert the heathen, he will do so without your help or mine." But William Carey refused to let the fire of his enthusiasm be dampened by such a response, and eventually he did leave England for India where he did pioneer missionary work. It was his enthusiasm to reach the unsaved in India that helped him to endure countless obstacles and 15 years of missionary work before he had his first convert.

In conclusion, a vision will begin with a concern that something must change which usually leads to a season of prayer during which God develops the vision within you. When the timing is right to begin pursuit of the vision, investigate before casting your vision to others. Investigate thoroughly the conditions of things as they are right now and what can be done to improve those conditions. Envision its fulfillment and how it will be fulfilled and write the steps that will be taken to fulfill it. Once your thorough investigation is done, you are now ready to cast your vision to others. Your vision casting should involve clearly explaining the vision, presenting the vision in a visual way, explaining the benefits of fulfilling the vision, and finally why the timing is right to seek its fulfillment now. When your vision is cast effectively, it will create enthusiasm among those who will be helping you to fulfill it. They will be the very ones to say "Let's get started." Your words have the power to influence people to support your vision when that vision is properly cast out to them. A caught vision is a cast vision.

Challenge Questions:

1) Explain how a vision that God gives you will usually begin with a concern.
2) Why is it vital that you investigate thoroughly first before casting your vision to others?
3) What should your initial investigation consist of?
4) What are the four ways that you should cast your vision to others so it is caught?
5) What will be the result of casting your vision effectively?

Chapter 8

WHEN CRITICISM BECOMES CONSTRUCTIVE
Exodus 18:13-26

T HE VERY WORD "CRITICISM" PERHAPS makes most of us cringe. The first thoughts we think of when we hear this word are probably somebody saying something negative about someone else or about something they don't like. We think of put-down remarks, of gossip, of slander.

It seems like no matter where we go, what we read, or what we watch, we are constantly bombarded with words of criticism. There seems to be no way to escape its negative influence.

But even in the midst of all the negative criticism that we hear, there is also a positive criticism called constructive criticism. We don't hear much about it because it gets overshadowed by the negative criticism that is so prevalent today.

So what is constructive criticism? What makes it positive? How does it have a positive influence on others as compared to the negative influence on others that destructive criticism has? How can we know if the criticism we receive or give people is really constructive?

These are questions that will be answered in this chapter. So let's discover together when criticism becomes constructive.

Criticism Becomes Constructive When Given out of Concern

Exodus 18:13-18—"The next day Moses took his seat to serve as judge for the people, and they stood around him from morning till evening. When his father-in-law saw all that Moses was doing for the people, he said, 'What is this you are doing for the people? Why do you alone sit as judge, while all these people stand around you from morning till evening?' Moses answered him, 'Because the people come to me to seek God's will. Whenever they have a dispute, it is brought to me, and I decide between the parties and inform them of God's decrees and instructions.' Moses' father-in-law replied, 'What you are doing is not good. You and these people who come to you will only wear yourselves out. The work is too heavy for you; you cannot handle it alone.'"

As Jethro sees Moses judging the people from morning until evening, he offers Moses, his son-in-law, some sound advice. Jethro knew Moses' tendencies, his work habits, his strengths, and weaknesses. After all, Moses had worked for him for 40 years. So, he didn't hold back when he said, "You're not doing the right thing," and he tells him why in verse 18, "You and these people who come to you will only wear yourselves out. The work is too heavy for you; you cannot handle it alone." He was letting Moses know that he and all the people were going to wear out unless he utilized his time more wisely. So obviously the counsel that Jethro was giving to Moses was given out of concern for not only Moses and his health but also for the people.

It's when criticism is given out of concern that it becomes constructive. Such criticism has the other person's well-being in mind and is given to help the person not to destroy him. The person giving the criticism is able to see clearly something destructive happening in the other person's life that they themselves usually are not able to see and so the criticism serves as a wake-up call and an alert.

This is much like the weatherman who sees a tornado that is making a destructive path toward a town. The people in the town do not see the tornado yet or even know that it is coming their way. So the weatherman will have an alarm sounded to warn all those in the path of this destructive tornado to go for cover. The alarm they hear serves as a wake-up call and an alert.

I remember such a wake-up call that I received many years back from my wife. Our daughter, Brianna, was about three years at the time and I was a full-time pastor. I was passionate about what I was doing as a pastor and was pursuing my calling with all my might from early morning to late at night. During the day, I was either preparing sermons or lessons or doing repair projects and in the evenings was visiting or having counseling sessions. I thought I was doing the right things, but my wife was able to see that I was going to wear out if I didn't slow down and she also saw that because of my busyness, I had grown distant from my daughter. When she told me what I was doing, it stung at first; but I came to realize that her criticism was given out of concern not only for me and my health but because of the effect that it was having on our daughter. I'm glad she sounded the alarm for me.

You see it's the motivation in which the criticism is given that determines if it is constructive or not. Criticism that is given with the motivation of helping someone becomes constructive but criticism that is given to hurt someone is not constructive but rather destructive. Criticism that becomes destructive is usually motivated by a desire to get revenge on someone or is given out of jealousy. It does not have the other person's best interests in mind but rather seeks to tear them down.

Such criticism was displayed by Miriam and Aaron who spoke against Moses because of the Ethiopian woman whom he had married (perhaps, because she was of a darker skin). The real motive for their criticism, however, surfaces in Numbers 12:2 as they felt that Moses was monopolizing too much power and they felt that they should have an equal say in things. They could not deny that God had sometimes spoken by Moses, but it was plain to them that God had sometimes spoken by them also. Their criticism of Moses was motivated by pride and jealousy which made their criticism destructive, not constructive.

"Better is open rebuke than hidden love. Wounds from a friend can be trusted, but an enemy multiplies kisses" (Proverbs 27:5-6).

There are some who may be called friends but whose love is a hidden love. Their love is hidden because they will only tell us things that they believe we want to hear. They would rather flatter us with their words than be truthful and honest with us about things that they see in our lives that concern them. They go through life trying their best not to upset the apple cart.

A true friend, however, like Jethro was to Moses, will manifest their love openly to us by being honest with us when they see things in our lives that are starting to concern them. Their open rebuke is done from a caring heart that really wants to help us. They see us taking a course of action that is not good and out of concern they feel the need to warn us.

This is the value of having a true friend: their honesty with us can save us from a world of hurt and making bad choices that could cost us everything. Many times they are able to see things in our lives that are detrimental that we may be blinded to.

I like how Leroy Koopman describes speaking the truth in love:

The book of Ephesians says that it's not enough to speak the truth. We are to speak the truth "in love" (Eph. 4:15). Perhaps your husband irritates others when he cracks his knuckles in public. Tell him the truth-but tell the truth in love. Perhaps your wife irritates others when she laughs too loudly in public. Tell her the truth-but tell the truth in love. Perhaps a friend is inviting tragedy by becoming too friendly with a coworker. Tell your friend the truth-but do so with kindness. Perhaps the cult member who calls at your door is teaching a false and dangerous doctrine. Share your understanding of the truth with your caller-but do so in love, without nasty remarks and a slammed door.[1]

Criticism Becomes Constructive When it is Sound Advice

Exodus 18:19-23—"Listen now to me and I will give you some advice, and may God be with you. You must be the people's representative before God and bring their disputes to him. Teach them his decrees and instructions, and show them the way they are to live and how they are to behave. But select capable men from all the people—men who fear God, trustworthy men who hate dishonest gain—and appoint them as officials over thousands, hundreds, fifties and tens. Have them serve as judges for the people at all times, but have them bring every difficult case to you; the simple cases they can decide themselves. That will make your load lighter, because they will share it with you. If you do this and God so commands, you will be able to stand the strain, and all these people will go home satisfied."

Jethro here gives Moses sound advice on how to get his priorities right. He tells Moses that instead of teaching and advising the people one at a time, he should teach them as a whole group the ordinances and laws so they might know how to walk in God's will and do his work. This was Moses' main responsibility as the leader to the people. He also gives Moses wise counsel regarding how to delegate. He tells him that he should provide able and spiritually competent men to be rulers of thousands, and rulers of hundreds, and rulers of fifties, and rulers of tens; and let them judge the people in every small matter and any great matters that they couldn't resolve, they would then bring to Moses. By this means, they would bear the burden of the workload with Moses and he would be able to endure.

Something that is constructive builds us up, it is useful. Thus, constructive criticism will be advice that will be useful to the person it is given to and helpful. They will be able to take that advice and as they act on it, build up areas of their life that need attending to. By listening to the criticism they receive understanding.

Proverbs 15:32 says "Those who disregard discipline despise themselves, but the one who heeds correction gains understanding."

It's much like a person who is trying to install kitchen cabinets for the first time but can't get the doors to shut properly after they are hung. He has a professional look at them and he advises him that when the cabinets were hung, they were not in proper alignment. He then writes down detailed instructions on how the cabinets should be properly hung. The criticism he offered was constructive as he explains what was done wrong but also he gives helpful advice on how to fix it.

I have noticed in my own life that the advice I have received from those who were more experienced than I was at something was usually advice that has been very helpful. They were able to see clearly the mistakes that I was making and through years of trial and error in their own lives, were able to show me a better way to do it. Their instructions taught me more than I ever could have learned reading a how-to-book. This has helped me through the years to be open to such advice without taking it personally.

Criticism Becomes Constructive When it is Accepted

Exodus 18:24-26—"Moses listened to his father-in-law and did everything he said. He chose capable men from all Israel and made them leaders of the people, officials over thousands, hundreds, fifties and tens. They served as judges for the people at all times. The difficult cases they brought to Moses, but the simple ones they decided themselves."

Moses had good sense to take Jethro's advice. Pride could have kept him from it. He could have taken on the attitude that Jethro had no right telling him what to do. After all, he is the one whom God spoke to and revealed Himself to and so if he needs advice, he will go right to God to get it; he does not need an in law to come along and tell him what he should do. How easy it would have been for Moses to have reacted like this. Although he sought to justify himself at first, he did eventually hearken to the voice of his father-in-law, and did all that he said (v.24). Moses was able to make wise use of his time because of his willingness to listen to the wise counsel of Jethro. I believe what enabled Moses to do so was that he realized that the advice was given out of concern and that it was sound advice—so the criticism he received was constructive.

How we receive advice and criticism from others is so critical. It's easy to take the criticism personally and think, "If they only knew what my schedule was like or if they were in my shoes, they would be more supportive of me." However, when we can come to the conclusion that the criticism was given out of love and concern, there is no reason to take it personally. It takes real humility to listen to what others suggest, to look inward, and examine what changes could be made. This is the type of humility that Moses obviously had. The Bible refers to Moses as the most meek man on the earth.

It also takes real wisdom to listen to advice as we realize that others can sometimes see more clearly what is happening in our lives than what we can.

"The way of fools seems right to them, but the wise listen to advice" (Proverbs 12:15).

So instead of reacting defensively when people give us advice and criticism, we should first stop and examine the criticism they are giving—is it given out of concern for our well-being and is it sound advice? This will help us to determine if the criticism is constructive or not and should be heeded to.

As a matter of fact, why wait for others to come to us with advice and criticism? Periodically, go to someone we trust and we know will be honest with us and ask for their opinion if they think we are out of balance with anything in our lives. Our initiative for seeking their advice will give them the courage to be honest with us. I believe we all need accountability partners, people who will not only be honest with us when we ask their opinion but who will hold us accountable to changes that we commit to making.

So criticism can be a good thing sometimes when it comes from someone who really cares and it is sound advice. I wonder in my own life if I have received criticism that was meant to help me but because I took it the wrong way, never was benefited by it. Yes, there is a negative criticism that is destructive but there is also a positive criticism that is constructive. I hope this chapter has helped you to see the difference so that you may be open to criticism that can help you and give you understanding. Constructive criticism influences us only when we are willing to receive it and it has an influence on others when we are the ones who are giving it to benefit someone else.

Challenge Questions:

1) Why is it true that it is the motivation in which criticism is given that determines if it is constructive or not?

2) How can receiving constructive criticism be helpful to you?

3) Do you usually react defensively when someone tries to give you advice and criticism? What can you do to determine if the criticism you are receiving is really constructive and should be heeded to?

4) Will you accept this challenge and go to someone you trust and who knows your tendencies and ask them if they notice anything out of balance in your life?

Chapter 9

INSPIRING WORDS LEAD TO GREATNESS

II Timothy 1:1-7

EPHESIANS 4:29 STATES, "DO NOT let any unwholesome talk come out of your mouths, but only what is helpful for building others up according to their needs, that it may benefit those who listen." Unwholesome talk refers to words that are worthless, unprofitable, of no use to anyone. Thus, in their relation to others, they do nothing to encourage or build others up. They are idle words that serve no purpose. Words that build others up, however, are words that have worth and are profitable because such words edify and bless those who hear them.

Our words really do carry power and influence. Words have a powerful influence over people ultimately shaping how one behaves, feels, and acts throughout life. Inspiring words lead to greatness, they can inspire others to do things that they thought they could never achieve. Most of the people in history who accomplished great things had someone who believed in them and inspired them to greatness.

But I have often wondered how many people never reached the potential that God had for them because no one ever told them that they believed in them or that they could become something and accomplish something great.

In this chapter, we will examine how Paul's inspiring words to Timothy led to greatness in Timothy's life.

Speaking Blessings into People's Lives.

II Timothy 1:1-2: "Paul, an apostle of Christ Jesus by the will of God, in keeping with the promise of life that is in Christ Jesus, To Timothy, my dear son: Grace, mercy and peace from God the Father and Christ Jesus our Lord."

In verse 1, Paul writes that he was called to be an apostle in accordance with the divine will and purpose of God. He further writes that he was called to this apostleship for the great purpose of sharing the gospel—that message of hope in which God has made a promise of life to mankind through faith in the Lord Jesus Christ.

In verse 2, we read to whom Paul writes this letter—to Timothy, whom he considered to be his dearly beloved son. Notice here the affection that Paul had for Timothy as he regarded him as his own son.

It was because of Paul's strong feelings of concern for Timothy's well-being that prompts him to speak God's blessings into his life with the inspiring words, ". . . Grace, mercy, and peace, from God the Father and Christ Jesus our Lord." Grace, mercy, and peace are all blessings that God bestows on those whom He desires to show favor and to bless. Thus, Paul was speaking God's blessings into Timothy's life.

We see the importance of speaking blessings into people's lives in the Old Testament where the father before he died would speak blessings into the lives of his children. The oldest son would receive the greatest blessing as he would be recipient of the main inheritance. Thus, the speaking forth of such blessings became a determining factor in the destiny of the children and what they would possess in the future. Is it any wonder that Jacob went to such great lengths to steal Esau's inheritance from him through deception.

As parents, our words today can also have great influence on our children into determining their future. When we tell our children that we believe in them and that they have what it takes to succeed, we are speaking blessings into their lives because such words will motivate them to accomplish more with their lives. However, we as parents can also fall into the trap of always downplaying our children's performance. "Why can't you get better grades?" "You never clean your room right." "Couldn't you have run faster in that race?" Such words can crush the spirit of our children and cause them to lose their self-value. They can also cause feelings of insecurity and inferiority to enter their lives, causing them to never reach the potential that God has planned for them. As parents, we want to bless our children's future, not curse it.

Joel Osteen writes on drawing out the best in others:

> We can either draw out the best in people or we can draw out the worst. I read 75 percent of people in prison reported that either their parents or their guardians had predicted in childhood where they would end up. The wrong seeds were planted. Low expectations were set. When a child is told to expect the worst, the child becomes the worst. I often wonder what would have happened if somebody would have told those people in prison that they might one day be doctors or entrepreneurs or great teachers. There's no telling where those inmates might have ended up if only they'd had people builders in their lives. If only someone had believed in them and taken the time to draw out their gifts, to listen to their dreams, to see what they

were good at, and then encourage them to be the best they could be. If only someone had given them permission to succeed instead of a prediction that they would fail.[1]

So our words become inspiring to others when we speak words of blessing into their lives. This is easy to do when we have tender affection for someone like Paul did for Timothy and we have a concern for their well-being. Just think how much stronger marriages would be and relationships in general if people would practice this principle of speaking God's blessings into one another's lives.

"May those who pass by not say to them, 'The blessing of the Lord be on you; we bless you in the name of the Lord' (Psalms 129:8)."

The fact is when we speak blessings into people's lives, we get blessed too. Jesus said that "it is more blessed to give than to receive." It's almost kind of ironic, but when we seek to bless others with our words, we get blessed in return. The blesser becomes blessed. Of course, this is not the reason why we speak words of blessings into people's lives, but it is the result of doing so.

A Necessary Condition to Inspire Others

II Timothy 1:3-4: "I thank God, whom I serve, as my ancestors did, with a clear conscience, as night and day I constantly remember you in my prayers. Recalling your tears, I long to see you, so that I may be filled with joy."

In verse 3, Paul writes that after the example of his ancestors, he served the same God. He saw no conflict between his service to God as a preacher of the gospel and the service to God given by ancestral Jews before Christ came. His service to God and theirs was motivated by a desire to please

God. Thus, to Paul he served the same God that his forefathers served. He was taught how to serve God by seeing it modeled in his forefathers.

Paul adds that he serves God with a clear conscience. He could do so because there was nothing in his life God was displeased with, there were no barriers between him and God. He was assured of this because his conscience was not grieved in any way. No wonder Paul could have such confidence to pray to God and to boldly proclaim the gospel.

Paul, however, is not sharing this with Timothy so Timothy might think he was something special but rather to reinforce to Timothy how sincere his concern was for him, a concern that came from a clear conscience.

He seeks further to reinforce his concern for Timothy by sharing with him that he constantly prayed for him night and day. Isn't it true that when we truly develop a burden for someone and their welfare that we carry that burden with us all day long and it motivates us to constantly pray for them? Paul wrote "My dear children, for whom I am again in the pains of childbirth until Christ is formed in you" (Galatians 4:19).

Paul then shares with Timothy how greatly he longed to see him being mindful of the tears that Timothy shed when they last parted. He further relates to Timothy that it would bring him much joy to see him again, his truly beloved friend whom he loved and cared for so much. He mentions this to him in hopes that Timothy could come to Rome and visit him in prison.

Everywhere we go, people are hurting. People are discouraged because of broken dreams. Others have made a mess of their life because of their mistakes. Many have lost hope of things getting better because of financial ruin. Such people don't need somebody to judge and criticize them, or to tell them what they're doing wrong. Rather they need someone to show them God's mercy and love, someone who will simply take time to empathize with them and show that they genuinely care. God has given us the ability to empathize with other people's pain so we feel their pain but only if we don't close our hearts to compassion because of our own selfishness.

"Continue to remember those in prison as if you were together with them in prison, and those who are mistreated as if you yourselves were suffering" (Hebrews 13:3).

"Carry each other's burdens, and in this way you will fulfill the law of Christ" (Galatians 6:2).

The fact is before anyone will accept our ministry of grace to them through our inspiring words, they must first be convinced that we care for them. There is a popular saying that people don't care how much you know until they first see how much you care. Before we seek to inspire people with our words, let them know how concerned we have been for their welfare and that we have been praying constantly for them and also what their friendship means to us. When they can accept first that our concern for them is genuine, it allows them to open their hearts up to our inspiring words.

Before Christ sought to encourage Peter with inspiring words that Peter would one day feed his spiritual sheep, he first made supper and served Peter fish. Christ knew that Peter felt ashamed over his betrayal and before he would accept his inspiring words, he needed to know first how much He still cared for him and considered him a friend.

When I was serving a pastorate in southern Illinois, I had searing pains in my side under my rib cage for weeks. As the pain got to be unbearable, I finally went to the doctor who told me that my spleen would need to be taken out.

When my overseer heard this, he called me on the phone and wanted to know if he could drive down to have prayer with me – a drive of about 5 hours. I told him that would not be necessary, that he could just pray with me over the phone. But he insisted that he really wanted to be there with me and anoint me with oil and pray for healing. And the very next day he did.

What that proved to me was how much my overseer really cared for me. And after that, whenever he would seek to inspire me with his words to become the best pastor that I could be, I really listened and took to heart what he told me because I knew those were words being spoken by someone who really cared and really wanted to see me succeed.

The Value of Compliments

II Timothy 1:5: "I am reminded of your sincere faith, which first lived in your grandmother Lois and in your mother Eunice and, I am persuaded, now lives in you also."

Paul now seeks to build Timothy up through complimentary words. He writes to Timothy that he remembers his faith and how it is sincere and genuine like the faith that dwelt first in Lois, his grandmother, and in his mother Eunice. There were times in their travels together where Timothy's faith was tested because of the opposition they faced and possible dangers as they went from city to city sharing the gospel. Yet despite the opposition and dangers, Timothy maintained his faith in God and proved that his faith was sincere and genuine. It is said that a person will never know how sincere and genuine their faith really is until it becomes tried and tested. Well, according to Paul, Timothy had passed the test.

I Peter 4:12, "Dear friends, do not be surprised at the fiery ordeal that has come on you to test you, as though something strange were happening to you."

Paul's complimentary words to Timothy of his genuine faith was exactly what Timothy needed to hear during a very trying time in which he was doubting his ability to be a pastor.

Compliments are expressions of approval or courtesy to one who has performed well. They have the power to build people up and inspire them. Compliments are needful because there is an innate desire within each person to be told from time to time that they are worthwhile and count for something.

However, we should never give someone compliments merely for the sake of giving them a compliment but we must be sincere when we do so. Everybody has positive traits so it is just a matter of focusing on the positive things in people's lives. Therefore, we can always find something in people to compliment.

Dale Carnegie relates from his best-selling *How to Win Friends & Influence People* that when the praise we give to people is specific, it comes across as being sincere:

> Everybody likes to be praised, but when praise is specific,
> it comes across as sincere–not something the other person
> may be saying just to make one feel good. Remember, we
> all crave appreciation and recognition, and will do almost
> anything to get it. But nobody wants insincerity. Nobody
> wants flattery.[2]

Look for a positive trait in that person's life that we are seeking to inspire with our words and vocalize it to them. Be specific about the positive trait. The fact is we can think good thoughts about people all day long but it's not going to do them any good unless we verbalize it to them.

If your wife cooks a wonderful meal, tell her why the meal was so good. If the waitress provides you good service, don't just think it but tell her that she did a great job in taking care of you. It's letting that person at church know how their ministry has touched your life.

Our wives especially like it when we give them descriptive praise. Instead of telling your wife that her dress was pretty, she will appreciate your praise more if you tell her why her dress is pretty. Instead of just telling her that you love her, tell her the reasons why you love her. A husband who compliments his wife with descriptive words will go a long way in making her feel valued.

Our attitude should be: Who can we build up with our words today and help them to believe in themselves even more? Our goal for each day should not just be to do what will make us feel better about ourselves but rather what can we do to make others feel better about themselves.

Proverbs 16:24 says, "Gracious words are a honeycomb, sweet to the soul and healing to the bones."

Gracious words are words that bring pleasure to people; it makes them feel good about themselves. Such words bring sweetness and health. It is said that the greatest hunger in the world is the hunger for appreciation. Have you ever noticed that usually after you give someone a compliment, how their whole countenance seems to light up and it brings a smile to their face?

Inspiring People to Rise Above Their Obstacles

II Timothy 1:6-7: "For this reason I remind you to fan into flame the gift of God, which is in you through the laying on of my hands. For the Spirit God gave us does not make us timid, but gives us power, love and self-discipline."

Timothy was facing tremendous difficulties and challenges as the pastor of the church at Ephesus which at that time was the mother church. The church there had become infiltrated with false teachers who were teaching the false doctrine of Gnosticism and there were elders trying to override Timothy's role as a pastor since he was young. These situations were causing Timothy to become timid and thus ineffective in his role as pastor.

Thus, Paul here seeks to challenge Timothy to rise above his timidity to accomplish God's purpose for his life. He reminds Timothy of the time that he was ordained into the ministry. Paul had united with the members of the presbytery in laying hands upon Timothy in appointing him to the sacred office of pastor. So Paul reminds him of this ordination because it meant that the elders had confidence in him as a capable minister.

Thus, based on this fact, Paul seeks to inspire Timothy to become zealous again (stir up, fan the flame) in his role as a pastor and not allow the spirit of fear or timidity to quench that fire in his spirit.

In the face of the opposition that Timothy was facing in the church, Paul challenges him to be bold and not be afraid. He tells him that his gift to pastor is to be characterized by power, love, and self-discipline. Timothy would need power to endure hardships in his ministry, power to preach and teach with the Spirit's anointing, power to face opposition with boldness. Timothy would need love to correct those in error with meekness and to be longsuffering towards those who opposed him. He would need self-discipline in keeping his own flesh under subjection.

Well, Paul's words did inspire Timothy because he did become a great pastor and a bold and confident leader. The church at Ephesus that had been overrun with false teaching and control issues became a strong church under Timothy's leadership and strong preaching.

Most people will not reach their full potential without somebody else believing in them. Thus, we should always be seeking to challenge people to reach for new heights. Don't focus on people's weaknesses but instead focus on their potential and what they can become. Everywhere Jesus went He saw people the way that they could become. He saw their potential. When people are around us, they should feel challenged and inspired. Our attitude should be: Who can I encourage today and inspire to overcome their obstacles to succeed in life?

"The Sovereign Lord has given me a well-instructed tongue, to know the word that sustains the weary. He wakens me morning by morning, wakens my ear to listen like one being instructed" (Isaiah 50:4).

It's our inspiring words that can challenge people to rise above their obstacles to accomplish great things for their lives. When we express positive expectations in people, it will help them to get refocused on what their purpose really is and enables them to step out in faith to accomplish that purpose despite the obstacles before them. Such words may sound like, "I believe that you can succeed in that new job," "I believe you can break that habit," or "I believe you are anointed to grow that ministry." Even after Peter's repeated failures and denials, Jesus told him that he would lead God's people.

When my daughter was around 7 years old, she was struggling with her spelling tests and we could tell that she was growing frustrated.

Instead of criticizing her for the low grades she was getting on her tests, we instead took the approach of telling her that we believed in her and she had the potential to get good grades. After our words of confidence in her, we could see that she was determined to learn those words during the week because now somebody believed in her and she didn't want to let us down. Her grades on her spelling tests gradually improved to where she was even getting perfect scores.

Your belief in people and their potential enables them to have belief in themselves. Your positive expectation in them motivates them to accomplish great things in their lives because people have a natural tendency to try and live up to the expectations that people have of them. Since that person has faith in them, they don't want to let them down. In the business world, companies that express positive expectations in their workforce will usually get the most production out of those workers.

After I accepted Christ into my life, I accepted my call into the ministry and was asked to preach a mini-sermon on a Wednesday night service. I prepared all week long for that sermon and when I got up to speak, I had four pages of notes. I thought for sure it would take me thirty minutes to preach all of that.

Well, when I got up there, I froze with fear as I looked out on the faces of the ten or so people in the congregation. Instead of preaching, I read my notes as quickly as possible and within five minutes was done with my message and then sat down. In a sense, I was relieved that it was over but also embarrassed that I had let my nervousness get the best of me.

After the service, an elder in the church came up to me and said that I ought to consider another occupation because I would never be a great preacher. His comments made me feel even worse and made me think that maybe he was right.

When everyone else had left that night, my pastor came up to me and told me that he saw something in me that God could use and that I had the potential to be a great minister of God and preacher someday. His positive words of belief gave me the courage and fortitude to not give up but to seek even more to become the best minister that I could be. His belief in me helped me to believe in myself and since that day, I have been ministering God's word for over 28 years.

Let's look for ways to inspire people to rise above their obstacles to accomplish great things. Let them know that you believe in them and that they have what it takes to succeed. Be specific in your compliments to people and they will know that you are sincere. Seek to bless other people with your words and you will be blessed too. Your inspiring words could be the very thing that someone needs to hear to rise to greatness in their life. They just needed to know that someone believed in them. Yes, our words do have influence on others when they inspire them to rise to greatness.

Challenge Questions:

1) When you speak blessings into people's lives, what effect can this have on their future?
2) Before others will accept your inspiring words on their behalf, what must they be convinced of first?
3) Do you find it easy to give others compliments? Why is it important that your compliments be specific in nature?
4) Relate how your inspiring words can challenge people to rise above their obstacles to accomplish great things for their lives?

Chapter 10

WORDS OF WISDOM
John 4:1-30

I F YOU ARE READING THIS book and have not accepted Christ into your heart, the wisest way to use your words right now is to confess and accept Christ into your heart as your Lord and Savior. The Bible says "If we confess our sins, he is faithful and just and will forgive us our sins and purify us from all unrighteousness" (I John 1:9). Confess to Christ that you are a sinner and that you are sorry for the sins that you have committed and that you want to make Christ the Lord of your life. If you do so sincerely from your heart, Christ will be true to His word and He will forgive you of all your past sins. The words of your confession become proof of the faith in your heart. "If you declare with your mouth, Jesus is Lord, and believe in your heart that God raised him from the dead, you will be saved. For it is with your heart that you believe and are justified, and it is with your mouth that you profess your faith and are saved" (Rom10:9-10). This is the wisest decision you could ever make and will allow you to apply the other principles you have learned in this book more effectively.

If you have already accepted Christ as your Savior, then the wisest way for you to use your words right now is to witness and lead people to Christ. But to do so will require wisdom.

Proverbs 11:30 states that ". . . and the one who is wise saves lives."

This scripture tells us that it takes wisdom to lead people to Christ. Those that would win souls have a need for wisdom and those who do win souls show that they are wise.

Wisdom has been defined as insight into the true nature of things, the ability to discern modes of action with a view to their results. One of the best definitions that I have ever heard of wisdom is that it is the right application of knowledge.

To be effective at soul winning requires that we have not only knowledge of salvation scriptures, but also how to rightly apply those scriptures in leading one to Christ.

Jesus is our example of how to use wisdom in witnessing as we see in His witness encounter with the Samaritan woman at the well.

In this chapter, we will show you how you can apply wisdom in your witness encounters that will enable you to not only discern when there is an opportunity to witness but also what wise approaches to take when witnessing with your words.

Discerning the Opportunity to Witness

John 4:1-4—"Now Jesus learned that the Pharisees had heard that he was gaining and baptizing more disciples than John—although in fact it was not Jesus who baptized, but his disciples. So he left Judea and went back once more to Galilee. Now he had to go through Samaria."

When Jesus left Judea, He was departing to go up to Galilee. Samaria lay between Judea and Galilee and thus passing through Samaria would have been the easiest and quickest route to go from Judea to Galilee. The Jews, however, would take the long way around Samaria because to them its land was unclean. Jesus, however, felt the need to go into Samaria.

Through wisdom, He discerned that there was a spiritual need there He needed to attend to, even though it didn't make rational sense for Him to go into Samaria. In going there, He risked the chance that His closest followers might reject Him and He postponed going up into Galilee where He possibly had some important business to take care of and where the people loved Him and where most of His miracles were done.

Spiritual wisdom and rationalization do not mix well together when it comes to witnessing. Rationalization causes one to lean on their own perceptions and feelings and thus to pick and choose whom they will witness to and only when it is convenient for them. Spiritual wisdom, however, enables one to discern opportunities to witness even when it doesn't make logical sense and is not convenient.

Many years ago, I was asked to go visit a lady in a nursing home. As I entered the nursing home, it had many hallways and was the first time that I had been there. I went up one hallway and could not locate the room I was looking for and as I was getting ready to go up another hall, I felt pressed in my spirit to go back down the same way that I had just come up. I began at first to rationalize how foolish this would be but I finally responded to God's leading.

When I got about halfway down the hall, a lady in one of the rooms to my left called out to me to come into her room and help her. At first, I thought she needed medical help but soon realized that she needed spiritual help.

When I entered her room, she told me that she had seen me walking up the hallway and figured that I was a preacher since I was carrying a Bible. She then prayed that God would send me back down so she could have a man of God lead her to salvation.

I knew then why God was pressing my spirit to go back down that same hallway. I opened up my Bible and shared with her the gospel and she wept her way to salvation. I learned from that experience to never question God's leading no matter how irrational it may seem.

Ephesians 5:15-16 says "Be very careful, then, how you live—not as unwise but as wise, making the most of every opportunity, because the days are evil."

This passage is saying that we are to walk wisely so that we don't miss any opportunities for doing good (redeeming the time) such as witnessing. The reason it gives is because the days are evil causing people's hearts to get harder toward spiritual things. Satan is working harder than ever to dull people's senses through such things as television, music, lust, materialism, and entertainment to the point that they are not the least bit interested in God or spiritual things. Our society is increasingly resembling the days of Noah in which every imagination of people's hearts were evil continually.

Because of this moral corruptness and the effects that it is having on people's hearts, it has become more difficult and our opportunities more limited to lead sinners to Christ. Thus, there is an evident need to seize every opportunity that presents itself to do good, such as witnessing.

Because of these limited opportunities to lead people to Christ, it is vital that we be able to discern those opportunities to witness because the fact is that opportunity may never come again. The business that

Jesus had up in Galilee could wait but the opportunity to witness to someone in Samaria may never come again.

God's timing is always perfect and He knows when a person's heart is receptive to the gospel. Thus, He attempts to make those divine connections of bringing a messenger of the gospel to that person. Right at that moment that God is leading us to witness to someone is when their heart is ready and receptive to the gospel but if we fail to discern that opportunity and not act it, that person's heart may never be open again to the gospel. That may be the last opportunity they will ever have to hear the good news.

"How, then, can they call on the one they have not believed in? And how can they believe in the one of whom they have not heard? And how can they hear without someone preaching to them? And how can anyone preach unless they are sent? As it is written: 'How beautiful are the feet of those who bring good news!' (Romans 10:14-15)."

Using a Physical Application to Explain a Spiritual Principle

John 4:5-14—"So he came to a town in Samaria called Sychar, near the plot of ground Jacob had given to his son Joseph. Jacob's well was there, and Jesus, tired as he was from the journey, sat down by the well. It was about noon. When a Samaritan woman came to draw water, Jesus said to her, 'Will you give me a drink?' (His disciples had gone into the town to buy food.) The Samaritan woman said to him, 'You are a Jew and I am a Samaritan woman. How can you ask me for a drink?' (For Jews do not associate with Samaritans.) Jesus answered her, 'If you knew the gift of God and who it is that asks you for a drink, you would have asked him and he would have given you living water.' 'Sir,' the woman said, 'you have nothing to draw with and the well is deep. Where can you get this living water? Are you greater than our father Jacob, who gave us the well and drank from it himself, as did also his sons and his livestock?' Jesus answered, 'Everyone who drinks this water will be thirsty again, but whoever drinks the water I give them will never thirst. Indeed, the water I give them will become in them a spring of water welling up to eternal life.'"

As the woman came to the well that day, Jesus discerned an opportunity to share the gospel with her by using a physical application to explain a spiritual concept. Jesus knew that this woman being from Samaria was probably not well-versed in the new way to salvation, so he used the physical application of something she knew well—the well of water—to explain the spiritual concept of living water which He came to give her.

Jesus used wisdom here as He made a comparison between the two to show her how much greater this living water was. He explains to her that whoever drank of the water from the well would thirst again, but whoever drank of the living water that He could give would never thirst again. The living water that He came to offer her would not remain stagnant like water in a well but would be as water that would continually spring up into everlasting life.

We use wisdom in our witnessing when we look for those points of transition in which we take a physical application of something that the person we are witnessing to is familiar with to explain the spiritual concept of salvation.

For example, if the person you are witnessing to is interested in former wars such as World War II, you could then relate to them that in the last days Jesus said that there would be a greater frequency of wars and rumors of wars. Another person whom you are witnessing to may be interested in gardening and you could then relate to them how we reap what we sow in this life, "For the wages of sin is death but the gift of God is eternal life in Jesus Christ our Lord."

This transition of taking a physical application to explain the spiritual concept of salvation is so vital because the natural man cannot discern and understand spiritual things. "The person without the Spirit does not accept the things that come from the Spirit of God but considers them foolishness, and cannot understand them because they are discerned only through the Spirit" (I Cor. 2:14). The fact is most people we witness to probably do not understand what we mean when we tell them that they must be saved. To them it means, "saved from what?" Thus, we need to start at their level of understanding and present the gospel in such a way that they will be able to understand and grasp it. This requires wisdom on our part as we find a way to share the gospel with them by using a physical application that they are familiar with first.

Avoiding Theological Debates

John 4:15-26—"The woman said to him, 'Sir, give me this water so that I won't get thirsty and have to keep coming here to draw water.' He told her, 'Go, call your husband and come back.' 'I have no husband,' she replied. Jesus said to her, 'You are right when you say you have no husband. The fact is, you have had five husbands, and the man you now have is not your husband. What you have just said is quite true.' 'Sir,' the woman said, 'I can see that you are a prophet. Our ancestors worshiped on this mountain, but you Jews claim that the place where we must worship is in Jerusalem.' 'Woman,' Jesus replied, 'believe me, a time is coming when you will worship the Father neither on this mountain nor in Jerusalem. You Samaritans worship what you do not know; we worship what we do know, for salvation is from the Jews. Yet a time is coming and has now come when the true worshipers will worship the Father in the Spirit and in truth, for they are the kind of worshipers the Father seeks. God is spirit, and his worshipers must worship in the Spirit and in truth.' The woman said, 'I know that Messiah' (called Christ) 'is coming. When he comes, he will explain everything to us.' Then Jesus declared, 'I, the one speaking to you—I am he.'"

As Jesus tells the woman to go call her husband, her response was that she had no husband. Jesus then tells her that she indeed had five husbands and the one she had now was not her husband. He tells her this to convince her that He was indeed greater than Jacob who gave her people the well of water since He knew all things about her even though He was a stranger to her. Thus, He certainly had the power to give her living water and everlasting life.

As Jesus delved further into her need for this living water of salvation, she got uneasy and attempted to get Him entangled in a theological debate over where one ought to worship: in Mount Gerizim where the Samaritans said was the proper place to worship or Jerusalem where the Jews said one ought to worship.

At this point, Jesus very easily could have debated with her and used Old Testament scriptures to prove to her that Jerusalem was the proper place to worship God since the Temple was there. However, this would not have been a very wise approach since this Samaritan woman was probably already feeling some resentment over the fact that the Jews would not allow the Samaritans to worship in their Temple. Thus, entering into a debate with her could have caused her to become angry and upset and thus prevented her from accepting this new way to salvation.

As we share the gospel with a sinner, it may make them uncomfortable as they come under conviction. This may cause them to attempt to steer the conversation into a theological debate.

I like how Barnes Notes describes how sinners try to change the conversation when it bears too hard upon their consciences:

> Nothing is more common than for sinners to change the conversation when it begins to bear too hard upon their consciences; and no way of doing it is more common than to direct it to some speculative inquiry having some sort of connection with religion, as if to show that they are willing to talk about religion, and do not wish to appear to be opposed to it. Sinners do not love direct religious conversation, but many are too well-bred to refuse altogether to talk about it; yet they choose to converse about some speculative matter, or something pertaining to the mere externals of religion, rather than the salvation of their own souls.[1]

It may be tempting on our part to enter into such debates and attempt to change their views on some things and clean them up first. However, in fishing you must catch the fish first before you attempt to clean them. It is our job to lead people to Christ and then let God clean them up. An unsaved person cannot understand spiritual concepts so attempting to win a debate with them over some theological concept will be a futile attempt that will probably just lead to contention and strife. Thus, we use wisdom when we stay focused on sharing the gospel which is the power of God unto salvation and not allow the conversation to get sidetracked into some theological debate.

Early in my ministry, I was holding a revival and going door to door during the day to invite people out for the evening services. As I came to one house, a gentleman invited me in and I discerned an opportunity to share the gospel. As I began to witness to him, I could tell he was coming under conviction and he attempted to get our conversation turned into a theological debate. We had differing views on what was required to be saved and I fell into the trap of entering into a theological debate with him over this; the debate ended up into a heated argument in which I was asked to leave. I learned a lesson from that experience to always try to stay focused on the central message of the gospel when witnessing. Debating with someone will never lead them to Christ but the sharing of the gospel message can.

Notice the wisdom that Jesus displayed here by not only avoiding a theological debate but redirecting the conversation back to the central message of the gospel. He tells her in verses 23 and 24 that true worshippers worship the Father in spirit and in truth for God is a Spirit.

In essence, He was telling her that true worship was not in a place but instead an attitude of the heart. He tells her that to truly worship God one must be able to call God their Father and worship Him in spirit. Thus, she needed to have a spiritual change of heart if she was to experience such a relationship with God. The fact is it is only after one is saved and their spirit is spiritually reenergized and made alive that they can now spiritually relate to God who is Spirit.

In our witnessing, the conversation may get misdirected but we use wisdom when we redirect the conversation back to the central message of the gospel. This is vital because it is the gospel (the good news that Jesus died for our sins so we can be saved) that is the power of God unto salvation (Romans 1:16). When the gospel is shared, God empowers that message by convicting sinners and showing them their need to be saved. The gospel message also shows them what they must do to be right with God (Romans 1:17).

One day I was talking to someone about the end times, a subject that they were deeply interested in. I saw a point of transition and asked the person if they were that convinced that we were living in the last days because of all the signs of the times, what was preventing them then from accepting Christ and being spiritually ready for His return. The person immediately tried to get me into a theological debate over how the dinosaurs could have gotten into the ark and did I think that God could have created everything in six days. My response was that they needed salvation first and then they would be able to get spiritual insights into God's word.

In verse 25, the woman does not seem to be satisfied with Jesus' answer and says that when the Messiah came he would explain everything to them. As the Samaritans acknowledged the first five books of Moses, so they expected, also, the coming of the Messiah. Probably, the Samaritan woman was expecting the Messiah to soon appear.

Jesus then uses wisdom here and avoids another theological debate by simply stating to her in verse 26 that He was that Messiah.

Barnes Notes explains why Jesus at this point made such a declaration:

> I am the Messiah. This was the first time that he openly professed it. He did not do it yet to the Jews, for it would have excited envy and opposition. But nothing could be apprehended in Samaria; and as the woman seemed reluctant to listen to him as a prophet, and professed her willingness to listen to the Messiah, he openly declared that he was the Christ, that by some means he might save her soul.[2]

Receiving Everlasting Life

John 4:27-30—"Just then his disciples returned and were surprised to find him talking with a woman. But no one asked, 'What do you want?' or 'Why are you talking with her?' Then, leaving her water jar, the woman went back to the town and said to the people,

'Come, see a man who told me everything I ever did. Could this be the Messiah?' They came out of the town and made their way toward him."

The Samaritan woman did drink of that living water that Jesus offered her and received everlasting life. How do we know? In these verses, we see where she left her water pot and returned to her city and proclaimed that Jesus was the Christ. She based her belief on the fact that Jesus told her things that she had done. Here was a woman who now had a new found joy in her life and she wanted others in her town to come and see for themselves the man who could give them living water. And the whole town responded. I believed they responded not just because of the message that she shared with them, but also because there was a definite change in her that could not be denied.

Charles Erdman in his Exposition on The Gospel of John delves further into whether this Samaritan woman really believed:

> Does the woman believe? Her action is more eloquent than speech. Six times Jesus has addressed her and each time she has made a reply. His seventh word declares him to be the Messiah; she makes no verbal answer, but we read that she "left her waterpot, and went away into the city, and saith to the people, Come, see a man, who told me all things that ever I did: can this be the Christ?" We do not know just how perfect her faith may have been; but, today, when a man or woman is found so interested in Christ that the daily task is for a time forgotten, and the one desire is to tell others about Christ, we are safe to conclude that faith is real and vital.[3]

It was a challenge for Jesus to lead this Samaritan woman to salvation because of her traditions and way of life but He was able to do so by using wisdom.

In these days we live in where people's hearts are becoming more influenced by the evil ways of our society, it's presenting more challenges for us to lead people to Christ and thus there is more of a need for us to use wisdom in our witnessing.

Who knows? That one person you lead to Christ may be able to influence many more people to come to the Messiah, just as this Samaritan woman did in her town.

A motto for witnessing that I read once goes: Reach every available prospect—By every available means—At every available opportunity.

Our words do carry influence in leading one to Christ when they are applied with wisdom. Truly, he that wins souls is wise.

Challenge Questions:

1) Why is it true that spiritual wisdom and rationalization do not mix well together when it comes to discerning opportunities to witness?
2) Why is it vital that you use a physical application to explain the spiritual concept of salvation when witnessing to someone?
3) Why is it more important to stay focused on sharing the gospel than trying to win a theological debate with someone you are witnessing to?
4) What evidence is there that the Samaritan woman received the living water that Jesus offered her?

NOTES

Chapter 1

[1] Joseph M. Stowell, The Weight Of Your Words (Chicago, IL: Moody Press, 1998), pg. 39-40.

[2] Warren W. Wiersbe, Be Mature (Colorado Springs, CO: David C. Cook, 1978), p. 98.

Chapter 2

[1] John R. McClure, Help For Our Infirmities (Cleveland, TN: White Wing Publishing House, 1989), p. 68.

[2] Terry Law, The Power of Praise and Worship (Tulsa, OK: Victory House, Inc., 1985), p. 126.

Chapter 3

[1] H. Norman Wright, The Pillars of Marriage (Ventura, CA: Regal Books, 1979), p. 162.

[2] Joel Osteen, Your Best Life Now (New York, NY: Warner Faith, 2004), p. 154.

Chapter 4

[1] Joyce Meyer, Battlefield of the Mind (New York, NY: Warner Faith, 1995), p. 34.

Chapter 5

1   John R. McClure, Help For Our Infirmities (Cleveland, TN: White Wing Publishing House, 1989), p. 98.
2   Charles R. Swindoll, David (Nashville, TN: W. Publishing Group, 1997), p. 106.
3   John Bevere, The Bait of Satan (Lake Mary, FL: Creation House, 1994), p. 179.

Chapter 6

1   Charles Capps, The Tongue—A Creative Force (Tulsa, OK: Harrison House, Inc., 1976), p. 129
2   Derek Prince, Faith To Live By (New Kensington, PA: Whitaker House, 1977), p. 96.
3   Ibid., p. 103.

Chapter 7

1   John Maxwell, Put Your Dream to the Test (Nashville, TN: Thomas Nelson, 2009), p. 124.
2   Ibid., p. 125-126.
3   Andy Stanley, Visioneering (Sisters, OR: Multnomah Publishers, Inc., 1999), p. 89.
4   Ibid., p. 99.

Chapter 8

1   Leroy Koopman, Beauty Care For The Tongue (Grand Rapids, MI: Kregel Publications, 1972), p. 45.

Chapter 9

1   Joel Osteen, Every Day a Friday (New York, NY: FaithWords, 2011), p. 230.
2   Dale Carnegie, How to Win Friends & Influence People (New York, NY: Simon & Schuster, Inc., 1936), p. 231.

Chapter 10

1   Albert Barnes, Barnes Notes (Grand Rapids, MI: Baker Books, 1998), p. 217.
2   Ibid., p. 219.
3   Charles R. Erdman, The Gospel of John (Grand Rapids, MI: Baker Book House, 1983), p. 49-50.